EDITOR: LEE JOHNSON

OSPREY MILITARY **WARRIOR SERIES** **3**

VIKING HERSIR
793–1066 AD

Text by
MARK HARRISON
Colour plates by
GERRY EMBLETON

First published in Great Britain in 1993 by
Osprey, an imprint of Reed Consumer Books Ltd.
Michelin House, 81 Fulham Road,
London SW3 6RB and Auckland, Melbourne,
Singapore and Toronto

ISBN 1 85532 318 4

Filmset in Great Britain
Printed through Bookbuilders Ltd, Hong Kong

Publisher's Note

Readers may wish to study this title in conjunction
with the following Osprey publications:

MAA 85	*Saxon, Viking and Norman Armies*
MAA 171	*Saladin and the Saracens*
MAA 89	*Byzantine Armies 886–1118*
Elite 3	*The Vikings*
Campaign 13	*Hastings 1066*

Artist's note:

Readers may care to note that the original paintings
from which the colour plates in this book were
prepared are available for private sale. All
reproduction copyright whatsoever is retained by the
publisher. All enquiries should be addressed to:

Scorpio Gallery
PO Box 475
Hailsham
E. Sussex BN27 2SL

The publishers regret that they can enter into no
correspondence upon this matter.

HISTORICAL BACKGROUND

To classical authors of the Mediterranean, the world was balanced perfection. The hot, dry, bright and civilised south found its opposite in the cold, wet, dark and barbaric north. The first inkling the Romans had that the two were not in perfect harmony was when the Cimbri and Teutones moved into southern Gaul in around 100 BC. The Romans understood these tribes to have originated in the Danish peninsula, but the nerve centre of threat to the Empire was located further north. The destructive Ostrogoths and Visigoths are described by Jordanes as economic refugees from the overcrowded Baltic island of Gotland.

This Scandinavian dimension to the barbarian menace survived the collapse of the Roman Empire. The Frankish successor state, the main inheritor of Roman traditions, found the far northerners increasingly threatening as time passed. The expedition of Hygelac the Geat to the Rhineland, recorded by Gregory of Tours and in the anonymous *Beowulf*, appears to be an isolated incident. As the Carolingians gained control over central and northern Germany, and thus came into contact with the southern borders of Danish settlement, the Vikings enter into the historical record with what appears to be a sudden and catastrophic impact.

When describing Scandinavia on the eve of the Viking Age it is difficult to avoid spuriously dividing it into three nations; Danish, Norwegian and Swedish. This division is largely a product of medieval history. The major difference between the various Viking homelands was the linguistic one of East and West Norse dialects. This picture is further complicated by an early emergence of centralised monarchy in Denmark. Signs of state formation above the level of clan and tribe can be seen in *The Frankish Royal Annals*. When Godfred of Denmark submitted to Charlemagne it was, in the mind of the chronicler, on behalf of a unified Danish kingdom. The power of the early Danish monarchy is plain to see in the refurbishment of the Danevirke, a massive, pre-Viking line of fortifications separating Jutland from mainland Europe. Only a regime of some wealth and power could have initiated such extensive work.

The Frankish Royal Annals further note that

Norway before the rise of Harald Harfargi. The names of the more important minor kingdoms are shown in upper case. Kaupang was the only town of any size at this period, but was subject to seasonal population changes.

Godfred's kingdom included the area of Vestfold. Although the writer placed this overseas province in Britain it was in fact part of Norway. The Danish foothold in Vestfold can be seen as the beginning of Danish domination of Norway. It also led directly to the early emergence of a Norwegian monarchy under King Harald in the 9th century.

Early raids

When Norwegian Vikings first raided the European coast in the 8th century AD, their leaders were not kings, princes or jarls, but a middle rank of warrior known as the *hersir*. At this time the *hersir* was typically an independent landowner or local chieftain. His equipment was usually superior to that of his followers. By the end of 'the 10th century, the independence of the *hersir* was gone, and he was now typically a regional servant of the Norwegian king. The *hersir's* equipment and status was now comparable to that of an immediate retainer of the Scandi-navian or English king, similar for example, to a Huscarl at the time of the battle of Hastings.

The earliest violent appearance of Norwegians on the coast of Britain is recorded in *The Anglo-Saxon Chronicle* for the year 789. Whether or not one views the murder of King Beorhtric's reeve (agent of the king) as an act of raiding, the chronicler confidently asserts 'Those were the first ships of Danish men which came to the land of the English'. In reality they appear to have been Norwegians from the district of Hjordaland.

The fact that earliest sources are written from the perspective of the Anglo Saxon Church may well have distorted our knowledge of the earliest phases of Viking raiding in England. We know that Offa was preparing the defences of Kent against pagan seamen as early as 792 and although our source is not specific we may suspect that these were Scandinavian pirates. The terms pagans, pirates and seamen had become synonymous with the Vikings by the end of the period. The apparent concentration of early raids on the monasteries of Lindisfarne (793) and Iona (795) probably conceals a picture of more widespread depredations. Continental raids show no such bias against the religious. The raiders off the Loire in 799

Raiding and settlement routes of the Vikings. Iceland, England and France were all colonised to various degrees and plundering was common in most areas shown on this map.

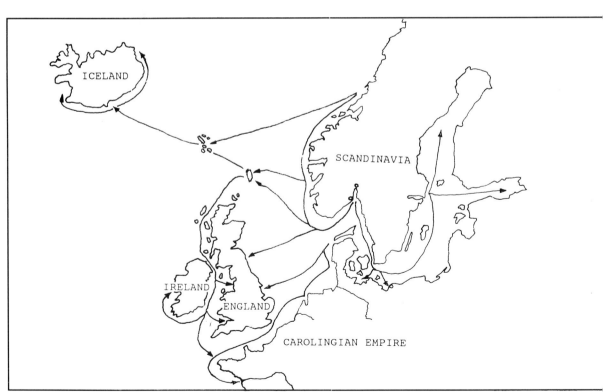

for example, are not noted as seeking out monastic communities. The Danish assault in 810 on the Carolingian province of Frisia and the subsequent attack in 820 may have been directed against important trading centres. Certainly by the mid 830s settlements of economic importance became the main targets of Viking attentions.

The emphasis in Old English records on the ecclesiastical bias of Nordic raids is one aspect of the cultural divide between Scandinavians and Christian Europeans in the 8th century. Even in Denmark, the most advanced of the three Scandinavian 'nations', the relationship of basic units of society to the elite class was very different to that in north-western Europe. The absence of a unified church or even a common religion weakened the possibility of a single national monarchy appearing.

The lack of a central authority meant that the use of violence by the individual, tribe or clan was institutionalised and accepted as inevitable. The increasingly powerful monarchies of the various English kingdoms were able to prevent violence by legislation which carried the sanction of the church. This intimate relationship of church and state limited aggression in a way Viking culture could not. Consequently when circumstance allowed Scandinavian intrusions into broadly peaceful continental Europe, the unlimited use of violence (a feature of everyday life in the Nordic lands) found lucrative outlets.

CHRONOLOGY

The decoration of this sword (Petersen type L) shows clear Saxon influence. Similar items are the river finds from *Gilling (Yorkshire) and Fiskerton (Lincolnshire). (By courtesy of the Board of Trustees, British Museum)*

89 Killing of King Beorhtric's reeve by Vikings.

92 Offa prepares defences of Kent against 'pagan seamen'.

93 Raid on Lindisfarne.

95 Raid on Iona.

99 Viking raiders off the mouth of the Loire.

10 Danish assault on Frisia.

30–850 Raids on the French coast and southern England.

35 Vikings land in West Country, defeated by Egbert, king of West Saxons.

. 850 Birth of Harald Harfargi.

851 First time a Viking army winters in England—at Thanet.

865 First English Danegeld paid by inhabitants of Kent.

866 Fall of York to Vikings.

c. 870 Harald Harfargi sole king of Norway.

c. 872 Battle of Hafrsfjord.

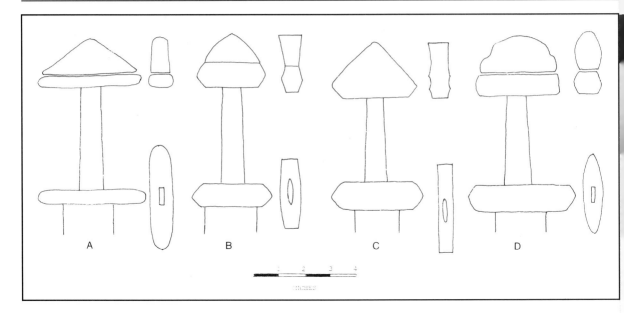

Petersen's Typology of Norwegian Swords. Cross-sections of pommel and guard are shown to the right of the profile where available. In each case the letter code applies to a particular find site. A: Bjertnes; B: Jarstad; C: Alstad; D: Ophus.

877 Fall of Mercia to Vikings.

879 Fall of East Anglia.

886 Treaty between Guthrum and Alfred. Siege of Paris.

895–905 Egil Skallagrimson born.

930–937 Resurgence of Wessex dynasty to unitary monarchy.

937 Battle of Brunanburh.

940–954 Intermittent independence for the Viking kingdom of York.

979 Accession of Ethelred II.

980 Renewed Viking raids on England.

c. 985 Death of Egil Skallagrimson.

991 Battle of Maldon.

991–1015 Extortion of massive Danegelds. Thorkel the Tall (Jomsviking) active in England. Sweyn asserts Danish mastery of England.

1016–1035 Reign of Canute. The 'Viking Empire' of the North sea.

1043–1066 Reign of Edward. The Battle of Stamford Bridge.

1085 Collapse of Sweyn Estridson's expedition to eastern England. The end of the Scandinavian threat.

TRAINING

In early Scandinavian society, the normal unit of warfare was the tribe. The sub-divisions of this were the family or clan. The Old Norse word for these extended family groups was *aett*. In the *Elder Edda* this is used to describe Angantyr and his sons, effectively a military unit (said to be berserkers) laid in a mass grave after their defeat and death. In a culture where the family was the fundamental combat group, training would, largely speaking, be part of everyday life.

Non blood-related loyalties were largely based around what is perhaps best termed the 'Gift Economy' which centred around the relationship between leader and followers. This relationship could often become elevated to a level more normal to bonds of kinship. In effect, it resulted in the formation of 'Artificial Clans'. Other versions of these simulated clans may have existed in groups of alienated, landless young men who gathered on the fringes of society and made a living by banditry and warfare. Such elements may have been the basis for the Norse stories of berserkers. In some sagas berserkers appear in groups of vagabond outlaws. In the society of early medieval Iceland, where so much depended on the family, landholding and well-defined rights of settlement, berserkers are seen as rootless outsiders.

Detail of spear socket with inlaid 'herringbone' pattern in silver. Several similar Norwegian examples are at the National Museum, Oslo. (By courtesy of the Board of Trustees, British Museum)

Axe of Petersen type B, found in the Thames near Whitehall. As with many 9th or 10th century weapons, it may have ended up in the river by accident, but more probably as the result of religious ritual. (By courtesy of the Board of Trustees, British Museum)

Several forms of the oath which legitimised the 'Artificial Clan' survive in the sagas. One appears in *Gisli's Saga*, where it is described in the following terms: A long sod is cut from the turf, with both ends still attached to the ground; this is held up by a spear with a pattern-welded blade, the shaft of which is so long that a man with an outstretched arm can just reach the rivets that hold the head in position. Those who are making the bond mingle their blood into the earth scratched up under the sod; kneeling they then swear an oath and shake hands, calling the gods to witness that they will avenge one another.

Another artificial extension of the family group was the system of fostering. Young children or adolescents could be sent to live in a separate household. Such arrangements did not normally exceed the boundaries of the clan, the most common form of fostering being to an uncle. Early Germanic languages have several words describing the very particular relationships that were established by this system. In the household of their foster-parent the duties of a young male would be identical to those of a son by birth—including training for war.

In the earliest phase of the Viking period all training would depend on these various forms of clan or pseudo-clan. Older members of the *aett* would pass on their knowledge of fighting techniques to the younger clan members either in formal training sessions or possibly by passing on oral traditions. The

latter might take the form of stories of past deeds or the lives of past heroes stressing the obligations of a warrior.

The particular brand of explosive violence which was the hallmark of Egil Skallagrimson was encouraged at an early stage by Thord Granison. Thord is described in *Egil's Saga* as young but older than Egil. Egil persuaded Thord to take him to the annual winter sports at White-river-dale in Iceland. When Egil fell into an argument with Grim Heggson which led to blows it was Thord who equipped and supported Egil for the slaying of Grim. At this time Egil was less than 12 years old. A similar incident occurs in the early life of Grettir Asmundson, although this does not end with a death, only threats of revenge. Grettir's first mankilling takes place when he is about 15 years old. If any reliance can be placed on these accounts a picture of society emerges dominated by violence as an everyday means of settling minor disputes. Adolescent males are not excluded from this aspect of life and extreme behaviour was modified by relatively mild correction. By these means the required mental attitude for a life of warfare was developed in the young. The semi-martial nature of the games which led Egil and

Sword typology (cont.). E: Vold; F: Hammer; G: Dale; H: Torshov.

Grettir to violence would give exercise and training in the handling of real weapons. The massive concentration in Old Norse sources on weapon-handling skills, recounted for the amazement and admiration of the reader, give us an insight into the importance of such abilities to the Viking warrior.

Large war bands

As the independence of the minor states in Norway was eroded, several options were left to those who did not wish to submit to the dynasty of Harald Harfargr. The first of these was settlement in another part of Europe where the rulers were less powerful or capable of being overthrown (for example in the Saxon kingdoms or the 'Norman' areas of Neustria). For the established middle-ranking landowners, with a certain amount of movable wealth and ambitions, colonisation of unpopulated Iceland was preferred. For the landless warrior the old form of raiding, in loose bands, was losing its viability. The defences of western Europe were able to turn back all but the largest hosts. These extended raiding bands were held together by allegiance to important figures like Rolf the Gänger. The formation of the Jomsvikings, an artificial tribe, was a reaction to this stiffening of resistance. New levels of organisation and training were achieved which allowed a penetration of the English kingdoms by this large war-band.

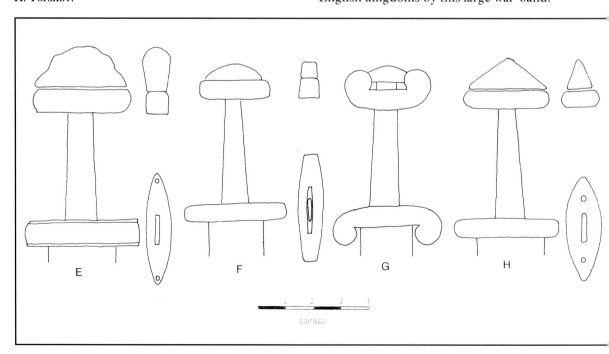

Icelandic records give a list of the laws which underpinned the Jomsviking's military society. The *saga of the Jomsvikings* records these as follows:

1. No man older than fifty or younger than 18 to be enrolled.

2. Kinship not to be taken into consideration on enrolment.

3. No man to run from an inferior opponent.

4. Jomsvikings to avenge one another as brothers.

5. No man to indicate fear by speech regardless of events.

6. Plunder to be held in common on pain of expulsion.

7. No one to stir up contention.

8. No spreading of rumours. The leader to disseminate all news.

9. No man to have a woman within the fortress.

10. No one to be absent more than three days.

11. The leader to have the final say in any dispute over kin-slaying which may have occurred outside the Jomsviking brotherhood.

Caution is required when attempting to treat the above as an exact account of the rules under which this early medieval unit operated. The laws are intended to supercede outside loyalties and replace them with new duties and obedience to the Jomsviking. Some parallels to individual laws can be found in *Halfs saga ok Halfsrekka* and echo some of the customs of the hird (Scandinavian territorial levy) as found in the *Hirdskra*. Jomsviking training went beyond weapon skills. The greatest innovation of this code was the application of older schemes and frameworks of loyalty to new conditions.

Although relatives were often recruited contrary to the laws, a form of selection appears to have been practised. Half of the followers of Sigvaldi Strut-Haraldson were turned away when their leader joined the organisation.

In its use of selective recruitment, the replacement of societal ties by new obligations to an artificial body and the imposition of a governing code the Jomsviking brotherhood has many similarities to more modern methods of organising military formations.

Individual weapon skill

The sagas recount numerous tales of individual weapon skill and daring. These deeds give an insight to the abilities which allowed the Norsemen to cut a swathe from the Caspian Sea to North America.

Skarphedin Njalson in a wintertime fight is reputed to have slid across an ice-sheet cutting down

Sword typology (cont.). I: Mosebo; K: Hedemarken; L: Dolven; M: Dovri.

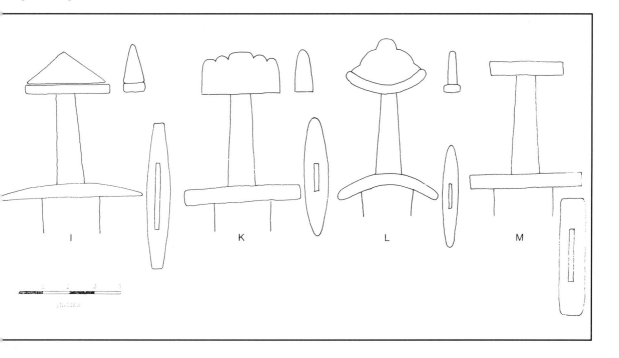

one man as he went and jumping over a shield thrown to trip him by a second. Olaf Tryggvason is said to have thrown two javelins at once with ambidextrous skill. On several occasions spears are caught in mid-flight and returned. The level of ability needed to carry out these exploits would need to be created and maintained by constant practice.

Archery practice, while not institutionalised as a legal requirement as in medieval England, is frequently implied. Einar Tambarskelve was able to shoot a headless arrow through a hide. This trick would be a training exercise requiring concentration, strength and accuracy. Hunting with bows would similarly hone the skills required in warfare.

The hunt encouraged quick thinking and reflexes and was an integral part of the way of life of the warrior class. It was a pastime, a means of destroying destructive pests and of providing food, as illustrated in *Grettir's Saga* where the hero encounters a troublesome bear.

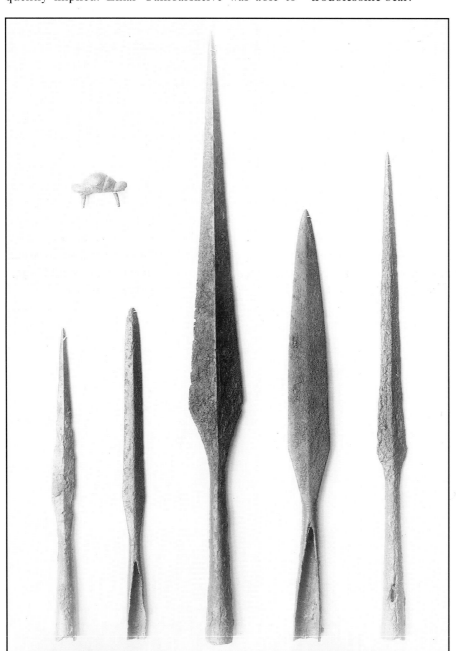

An assortment of Viking and Saxon spearheads of angular profile. At the top left, a pommel cap of Petersen type S; the two rods for attaching it to the upper cross-piece of the sword are clearly visible. (By courtesy of the Board of Trustees, British Museum)

TACTICS

The greatest strategic advantage held by the Vikings was their mobility, their freedom to operate within foreign territories. Unbound by treaty or convention the early raiding bands were able to give rein to the plundering instincts and use the violent tendencies, which characterised Scandinavian culture at this time, to achieve disruptive results out of proportion to their numbers. As the character of the Viking warrior changed and large-scale, semi-professional armies emerged it became important to safeguard the gains already made. As a consequence we find the Viking host of 876 swearing peace with Alfred on a sacred ring (which no one had succeeded in forcing them to do before) prior to the settlement of Northumbria.

Viking freedom of action throughout the period was based on the superiority of Scandinavian maritime ability. Alcuin expresses surprise that they were able to descend on the Northumbrian coast in 793. His shock probably owes more to the audacity of the pagans in attacking the monastery of Lindisfarne (one of the mother-houses of the Anglo-Saxon church) than any unexpected improvement in shipbuilding. More important than any superior boat-building technique was the skill of the Vikings as sailors. By a combination of sailing instructions passed down from generation to generation, advanced methods of navigation and excellent maritime skills, the Vikings were able to menace any part of Europe with enough water to float their shallow keels.

A favourite tactical ploy was the transfer of mobility to the land by the use of captured horses. This first occurred in England in 866 when a Viking force that had established a base in East Anglia, obtained mounts and were able to go overland to York. In 885 the raising of the siege of Rochester lead to the abandonment of the Vikings horses. Loss of mobility may have influenced the departure to the Continent that followed.

Despite the reasonably frequent use of horses in land warfare the Vikings were never natural cavalrymen. This owed less to the low quality of equine stock in Scandinavia than to military tradition, the accepted way of fighting a battle was on foot. Naval battles were made as much like land battles as possible. Ships would be roped together, either in a single line or groups, thus allowing a certain amount of mutual support between crews. The battle lines would then move head-on towards each other and after contact had been made a struggle of endurance would begin. Tactical subtlety was limited by the lack of

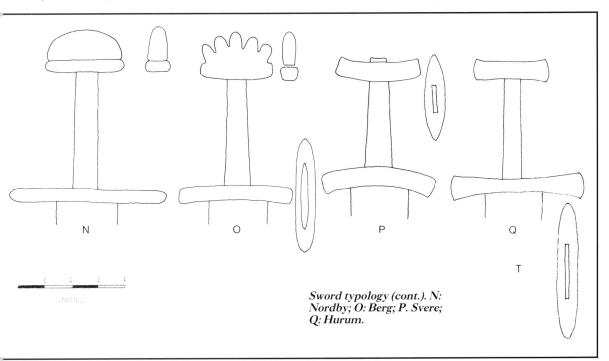

Sword typology (cont.). N: Nordby; O: Berg; P. Svere; Q: Hurum.

manoeuvrability, although ships that were able to break away from the main engagement were able to redeploy or even flee the fight. All naval engagements were fought close to land and in some instances the course of battle was affected by coastal features. In 896 three Viking ships were trapped by faulty mooring and destroyed by King Alfred's navy on the Hampshire coast. Suitably trained and equipped defenders were quite capable of matching the Vikings in their own element.

A form of positional warfare developed in late 9th century England with the Vikings and Saxons each making use of fortifications. These were often of a temporary nature, unlike the Trelleborg forts of the Danish homelands. Where they have been identified the Norse defences have always included a ditch and bank, and it seems likely that a wooden palisade would usually have been incorporated. The siege of Rochester in 885 may have involved the construction of lines of circumvallation. It is more probable that a less extensive fort was built outside the town's defences to act as a base for the Scandinavian attackers. In 894 King Alfred blockaded the two Viking camps at Appledore and Milton, acting as centres for raiding activities, and forced their abandonment. Remote coastal areas and islands were

captured by the Vikings to provide safe havens. Such maritime bases were sometimes unfortified, relying on their remote location, surrounding water and Norse control of the seaways. Occupation of such sites was often temporary, although re-use in succeeding seasons was common.

The Vikings have been credited with little tactical method but a large measure of ferocity. Two types of formation have been traditionally viewed as epitomising this tenacious crudity. One is the *skjaldborg* (usually translated as shield wall) and the other the *svinfylka* (swine array).

The shield wall

The shield wall was a tightly arrayed body of warriors who were close enough to overlap their shields in a mutually protective barrier. Representations of the deployed shield wall are rare. The Gosforth hog-back tomb suggests the interlocking of shields could be up to half their width. Gotland pictured stones seem to illustrate smaller shields overlapping by less than one quarter of the width. It might be reasonable to assume some variation of arrangement according to circumstance. The depth of a shield wall also appears to have been variable. When committed to the attack several ranks were customary, effectively a phalanx or column intending to break the opposing formation by weight of numbers. Several units could be deployed in mutually supporting *skjaldborgr*, which might also be positioned to mount surprise attacks.

Sword typology (cont.). R: Hedemarken; S: Vesterhaug; T: Utgaarden; U: Seim.

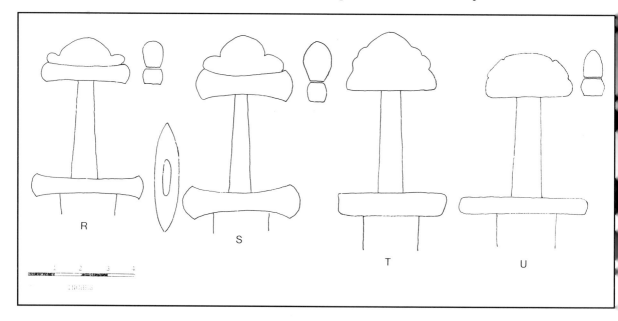

The shield wall was used defensively by Harald Hardrada at Stamford Bridge when he arranged his forces in a circular formation which lacked depth. The rear ranks of this formation locked shields in the same manner as the front rank. Hardrada's advice to his spearmen reflects what was probably standard practice for infantry formations facing a mounted charge (evidence for English cavalry at Stamford Bridge is inconclusive). The front rankers were told to set the butt of their spear to the ground and aim the point at the rider's chest, those in the second line were instructed to level their spear point at the horse. In addition the bodyguards of Tostig and Harald formed a mobile reserve intended to counter the more dangerous English assaults. This elite unit is said to have included archers who were commanded to give close support to the hand-to-hand fighters.

The swine array

The swine array was an offensive wedge arrangement, traditionally invented by the guileful Odin. It is more likely to have derived from the 4th–5th century late Roman legionary formation, the *porcinum capet* (swine head) rather than the teachings of a battle god. Icelandic descriptions suggest an arrangement in which the front rank was formed by two men, the second by three, the third by five, and so on.

The Vikings also used much smaller scale battle tactics. The deployment of fanatic units is discussed in the section on the Battle of Hafrsfjord. Other specialists were also employed. At the Battle of Svold Olaf Tryggvason had a bow-armed sniper, Einar Tambarskelf on board his flagship. Missile-armed troops, while rarely deciding the course of an action, were almost always present. Many descriptions of battles include poetic euphemisms ('Kennings') for arrows and throwing spears. The Old Norse language includes a word, *flyn*, specifically describing a throwing spear. Grettir Asmundson is said to have removed the rivet attaching the narrow head of a throwing spear to its shaft to prevent his intended victim from returning the missile.

Many weapons of the period would not neces-

Two spearheads of 9th or early 10th century. The one on the left is of broad-bladed Carolingian form which was imported by both Vikings and Saxons; the other is an example of Petersen type K. (By courtesy of the Board of Trustees, British Museum)

On the left a sword of Petersen type L, on the right one of type R. They frame two typical period spearheads. (By courtesy of the Board of Trustees, British Museum)

▶ *Sword typology (cont.). V: Ulvik; W: Bredvold; X: Hagerbakken.*

arily be well suited to tight formations. Without room for manoeuvre a long-handled axe swung with both hands is gravely handicapped. In the absence of surviving drill manuals it seems reasonable to assume that units of Vikings were able to vary their formation according to circumstance. Egil and Thorolf Skallagimson whilst harrying Courland split their forces into groups of twelve men. The Courlanders were unwilling to do more than skirmish with them and Egil's unit unaided was able to assault a small settlement.

The Courland incident in Egil's Saga also mentions the use of horns for signalling instructions to the dispersed sections of pillagers. We also read of signal calls for arming, to put to sea, to land, to attack and advance. Trumpets are also used to summon general assemblies in settlements. Such a variety of applications suggests that these signals were widely understood.

Flags and banners, for example the 'Raven' lost by Sigurd of Orkney at Clontarf in 1014, may also have been used to communicate the intentions of a commander. Standards could, at the least, mark the position of a general on the battlefield and give an idea of the direction of attack.

The sagas credit several outstanding Scandinavian generals of the early Middle Ages with a series of unlikely ploys and stratagems. These are folk-tales of unusual persistence often attached to the name of more than one leader. They range from feigned death, to gain entry to a besieged city claiming the need for burial, to the highly dubious use of wild birds as unwitting incendiaries. Even if none of these stories are true they represent an interest in disinformation and trickery which would not shame more systematic students of warfare.

Conventional forms of surprise attack were used. The winter assault on the Wessex royal palace at Chippenham was a master stroke which caught Alfred off his guard with almost fatal consequences. We see the Vikings mounting an offensive during a time when their enemy could reasonably expect them to be inactive, during a religious festival, from an unexpected direction using speed and overwhelming force. This has all the ingredients of an ideal surprise attack. It can be seen that without the benefit of formal military institutions the oral traditions of the Viking warrior still provided him with a range of strategic and tactical options.

LOGISTICS

Equipping and supplying a Viking army was a vastly different undertaking in the 8th century than it was later in the period. During the earlier part of the Viking Age decentralised power was unable to raise large forces without the consent of local war-lords.

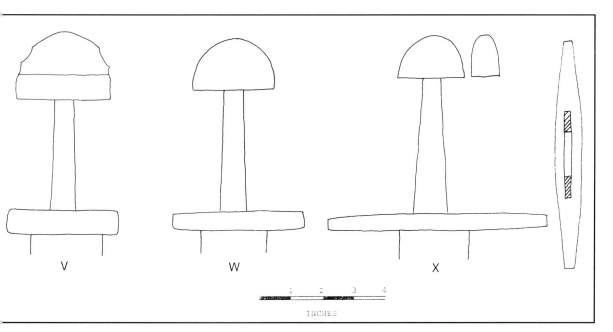

V   W   X

1   2   3   4
INCHES

These need not have been any more powerful than the *hersir*. Regional forces would have been raised and equipped within their own area of habitation. The later laws (Hirdskra) for the defence of Norway on a territorial basis are a late survival of this. The clan and tribe would each play their part in making it possible to mount an expedition. Organisation of war effort would rest with local landowners, who would also be the leaders of society.

The semi-legendary Ragnar Lodbrok, who was the leader of the earliest manifestation of the Great Army in England, appears to have laid claim to royal status. It would seem that, as with the ancient clan system, the reality of power lay with his *aett*. The Sons of Lodbrok (who may not have been blood relatives) were said to have conquered the northern kingdoms of the heptarchy in revenge for their 'father' having been executed in Northumbria. The Great Army worked on a series of interlocking loyalties which were not immutable. The campaigns of the army show that smaller groups were at liberty to conduct minor operations. One of the Lodbroksons was killed whilst raiding Devon in 878. The aim of this attack may have been to obtain land for settlement; in 876 Halfdan had divided Northumbria amongst his followers. It is equally possible that the

assault of 878 was intended as a *strandhogg*, a coasta raid for supplies and profit.

Two different systems of logistics can be seen a work. The opportunistic raiders established contro of land and agriculture in the political vacuum o Northumbria. In future the Norse kings of York wer to have a troubled but effective reign which, with some interruptions, continued until the mid-10th century. Armies were raised and equipped from thi area, sometimes supported by overseas Vikings. Th 878 incident may have had more important implic- ations, but the form of attack was that which had surprised Lindisfarne in 793, a swift descent on ar unprotected coast. The invaders would take whateve they needed from the region and move on. Unfortu- nately for their leader (according to the *Annals of St Neot* he was Hubba Lodbrokson) the nature of the defence had changed. Although the King of Wesse was himself a fugitive, the local ealdorman wa capable of meeting and destroying Hubba withou assistance from the central state. The outcome migh reflect the vagaries of warfare but some level o preparedness must have been necessary to defeat a force of 23 ships.

Fortifications

The militarisation of the English state, which mad the defeat of the raiders and the conquest of Englanc possible, depended on the network of fortification

Sword typology (cont.). Y: Skaaden; Z: Hafsten; A/E: Halsteinhov.

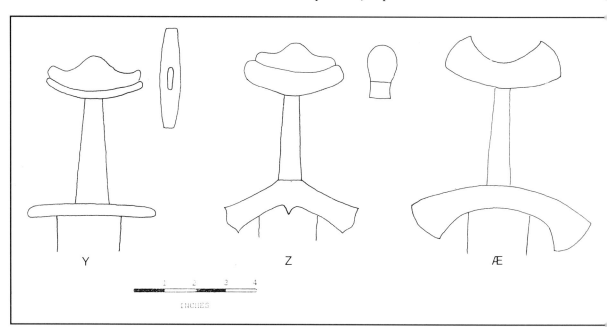

Y   Z   Æ

INCHES

which the Wessex dynasty was to build in the late 9th and 10th centuries. Positional warfare became more important in the later part of Alfred's reign as the Scandinavians attempted to defend their gains and break the last Saxon kingdom. *The Burghal Hideage* gives a picture of the way in which royal foundations were established every 20 miles or so. Supported by the resources of their area these were concentrations of regal power where mints, markets and refuge defences could be placed. The *burh* could act as a centre of control and resistance or as a base for further operations. In England these were often raised on the site of existing settlements, sometimes augmenting or adapting urban foundations of Roman origin. This phase of primary state formation has left similar traces in the archaeology of Scandinavia.

The most developed of the Viking kingdoms, Denmark, saw the building of a remarkable series of regional fortresses in the ninth century. These are named after the site of Trelleborg, although the earliest of the group appears to be the one at Fyrkat. The surprising regularity of their ground plan has led some writers to surmise that the Trelleborg forts were built to a strict military plan. Some have even suggested a modified 'Roman foot' in the measurement of the fortifications. This is about as likely as the completely bogus 'pyramid inch'. In fact these defensive works are not as innovative as they may first appear to be. The circular outline of the fortresses could be marked out with nothing more complex than a long rope attached at a single fixed point. Circular refuge forts of earlier date are known from the Baltic Åland Islands and from the Low Countries. The regularity of the internal buildings may reflect short-term occupation rather than a strictly military function. Interpretations that date these structures to the reign of Sweyn Forkbeard or Canute have stressed the military origin.

There can be little doubt that the Trelleborg forts were the product of a strong monarchy. They may even have been inspired by the *burh* system of Anglo-Saxon England. The purpose they served was the same—control of a developing country. The Danish conquest of England in the early 11th century was almost certainly made possible by well-organised logistic infrastructure provided by the Trelleborg forts of Denmark.

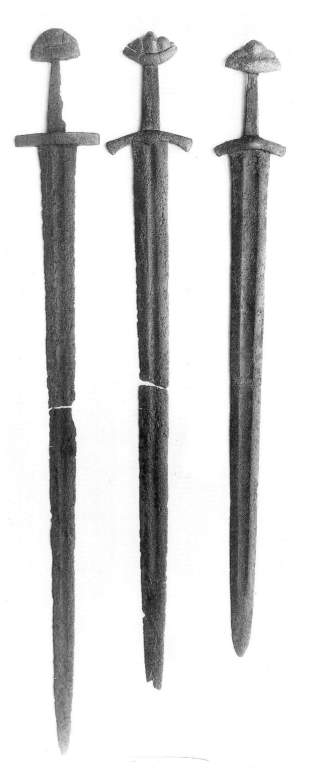

Three Viking swords found in British sites. Left to right: Canwick (type W), Edmonton (type Z) and Temple (type L.) (By courtesy of the Board of Trustees, British Museum)

17

Recruitment

The changing nature of the Viking warrior is exemplified by the shift from the regional method of recruitment and supply to the more complex national system. The crucial role of kings in this can be seen by the increasing importance of royalty in major projects. One of the largest longships ever built in the north was the *Long Serpent* funded by Olaf Tryggvason, who also contributed to the design. The logistics that supported the new, cohesive armies developed in some senses from the gift economy hence Tryggvason at the Battle of Svold is seen issuing swords to his bodyguard. One characteristic of good lordship in this period was the bestowal of fitting weapons.

The Jomsvikings were early participants in the Danegeld bonanza at the turn of the 10th and 11th centuries. Their main aim was the extortion of silver coinage. Thorkell the Tall had no inhibitions about changing sides as long as the flow of silver to his men was not interrupted. This was in fact their pay and although the financial practices of the age still tend to treat weight and quality of silver as the true value, the step to a currency based on confidence was only a short one. This immature version of economics was sufficient to support professional units like the Jomsvikings who could devote all their time to warfare.

The problem of supply was relatively simple for a Viking force. When not equipping in the homelands for an expedition they lived off the land by plunder, extorting directly from established authorities or settling in the lands they had destabilised. Transportation of supplies does not appear to have been by cart. Surviving examples of wheeled transport from Scandinavia are ceremonial and of a construction that could not have withstood extended use in a land of virtually non-existent roads. Written records from Iceland contain copious references to pack-horses.

THE VIKING IN BATTLE

The Battle of Hafrsfjord c.872

The only written records of the battle appear in Icelandic literature and were probably first composed over two hundred years after the events described. However the various sagas that touch upon the engagement are generally agreed in outline and

The mark of the master 'INGELRII', possibly spurious, is just visible inlaid in a different type of steel on this sword blade. The name is set in the blade by cutting an outline of the required letters into which white-hot wire is hammered. INGELRII was a famous blade smith of the middle of the Viking era. (BM Acc. No. 58, 7-1, 1404: By courtesy of the Board of Trustees, British Museum)

details. The importance of Hafrsfjord in Icelandic history lies in the impetus to emigration which followed the unfavourable outcome.

The forces engaged were those of Harald Harfargi, the would-be sole king of Norway, and a loose alliance of land owners of varying social standing from the northern and western areas of the country.

Harald Harfargi was the son of Halfdan the Black and through his father had inherited the minor kingdom of Vestfold. This area was of some importance as a trade route dominating the southern approaches to Norway (Kaupang was the principal entrepôt of the region). The large amount of level, fertile land around the Vik gave Harald certain advantages over his rivals. By a process of isolating and eliminating the petty kings of Norway one at a time, Harald had succeeded in absorbing or subduing Uppland, Trondelag, Naumdale, Halogaland, Maera and Raumsdale. If the *Saga of Egil Skallagrimson* is to be believed many people had already been forced into exile by the growing power of Harald. Of those who remained, 'many great men' resolved to rebel against Harald in defence of their right to unattached land-holding. They were supported in this by the still independent King Sulki of Rogaland. *The Saga of Grettir the Strong* informs us that Geirmund Swathy-skin, the overlord of Hjordaland, one of the few remaining independent kingdoms, was absent overseas. The names of additional allied leaders were Kjotvi the Wealthy and Thorir Longchin (the deposed king of Agdir).

Although Hafrsfjord took place at sea it bore little resemblance to a true naval action. Projectile weapons played little part in the course of the fight, which was resolved by a series of boarding actions. Neither was deliberate ramming in the pattern of classical naval warfare, a tactic employed at this time.

The precise size and composition of the two forces is not known, although Icelandic sources describe this as the largest battle ever fought by King Harald. *The Saga of Egil Skallagrimson* makes a particular point of listing the 'forecastle' men on King Harald's ship as these were to play an important part. Among them was the retained Thorolf Kvendulfson, the brother of Skallagrim Kveldulfson and uncle of Egil.

Items of Viking personal jewellery found at Chiseldown, Dorset: beads of glass, amber, crystal and paste. (By courtesy of the Board of Trustees, British Museum)

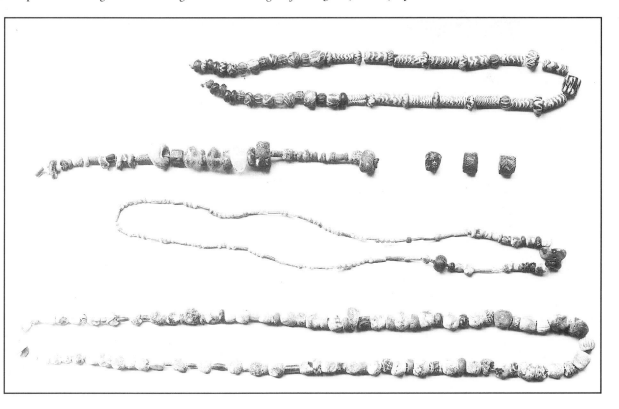

The group of hand-picked warriors in the prow of the ship appear to have been deployed behind an even more select group of berserkers. *Egil's Saga* gives the number of the king's berserkers as twelve, a figure which recurs in Norse literature when groups of these unusual warriors appear. In *Grettir's Saga* and in Sturluson's *Heimskringla* the berserkers are alternatively called 'Ulfhednar'. This may signify a fundamental difference between the more common form of berserker and the Ulfhednar. What is more likely is that the bear was extended to another animal noted for its ferocity, namely the wolf. 'Berserk' (Bear-shirt) and 'Ulfhednar' (Wolfskin) can be taken as terms for the psychotic fighting men of the period. Attempts to show that the Ulfhednar were uniformed in hides are groundless.

The intention of the king was to come alongside the ship of Thorir Longchin and strike directly at one of the foremost leaders of the allied force. King Harald ordered forward his Wolfskins, on whom no iron could bite and whose charge nothing could resist. Thorir Longchin was cut down in the onset. His followers' resolve collapsed, giving King Harald the victory.

Stripping this key section of the battle of any mystical elements we can see that a centralising monarchy is able to raise, equip and maintain a specialist fighting unit whose reputation is supernatural. At the crucial moment they are sent forward with a definite target whose elimination will cause the collapse of the opposition. Harald Harfargi's tactics might be relatively simple but the result was to influence the entire history of Norway and the very nature of the Viking warrior.

Brunanburh or Vinheath *c.937*

The image of the leader as the generous donor of valuables to his loyal followers remained one of the governing concepts of the early Middle Ages. Men fought not only for honour and glory but also for immediate and fitting reward. The form of such gifts might vary depending on the status of the recipient. To the young warrior of the immediate *hearth-weru*, or bodyguard, movable wealth, preferably in the form of ornamental jewellery, would be appropriate. One of the poetic descriptions of a good lord was 'ring-giver'. To an established noble or older veteran the right to land might be more important. As the gift economy changed towards one based on silver coinage a mercenary class seems to have emerged. The story of Egil Skallagrimson at Brunanburh reflects several aspects of this change.

Although the Wessex kings had established their supremacy over the lowlands, the peripheral areas of Britain, and in particular those under Celtic or Norse cultural domination, had not abandoned hope of independence. The similarity of Athelstan's position to that of Harald Harfargi in 872 is striking. That some fellow feeling, or at least a commonality of interest, existed between the two is shown by Athelstan's fostering of Hakon, the son of Harald.

The broad anti-English alliance had made strange political bedfellows of several lesser kings whose domains encircled the Irish Sea. These included Olaf the King of Dublin, a man of mixed Norse and Celtic descent who according to *Egil's Saga* was the prime mover of the allies.

The collapse of the accord of 927 between Athelstan and the northern kings began when the allies appear to have invaded Northumbria. The extent of their penetration into Saxon territory is unclear. Following the defeat of the joint Northumbrian earls Gudrek and Alfgeir, some form of harrying inside the northern part of Athelstan's realm seems to have taken place. To counter this Athelstan issued a challenge to the allies to meet within a defined area to decide who ruled Britain by combat. After such a challenge it was considered dishonourable to plunder further. Athelstan in his preparations for a northward march had sent word throughout north-western Europe that he wished to hire mercenaries. Egil Skallagrimson and his brother Thorolf, had been made aware of this whilst in the Low Countries and, we are told, were singled out by the king as suitable generals for the entire mercenary force. The part played by the hired warriors in this fight receives no mention in the Chronicle account, which instead highlights the contribution of the West Saxon and Mercian contingents.

Egil's Saga stresses the experiences of the Skallagrimson brothers in the fight and how their professional code determines everything from their equipment to the way in which they confront death. They are described as particularly well equipped both with defensive armour and specialised mail-piercing weapons. The fulfilment of their agreement with the king leads them into the thickest part of the battle where Thorolf and his men are abandoned by a Saxon earl named Alfgeir. In spite of this Thorolf is able to fight his way out of encirclement, cutting

Bone cross-piece of a sword from Dyfed, Wales. Despite the relative fragility of bone, Laxdaela Saga *describes such items being used in combat. (By courtesy of the Board of Trustees, British Museum)*

down Hring the Strathclyde British general in the process. Resistance from the allied army continues and during a lull in the fighting Athelstan gives his personal thanks to the Skallagrimsons. The saga theme of never trusting a king asserts itself. Athelstan insists on a faulty disposition of his troops, leading to the death of Thorolf, cut down in a surprise attack launched from a wood by the men of Strathclyde.

The survivors of Thorolf's personal unit are forced back but galvanised by the appearance of Egil in their ranks they rally, counterattack and put the Strathclyde contingent to flight. In the process the remaining Strathclyde British leader Adils is killed. The personal nature of the relationship between leaders and followers is revealed by the rout of the Strathclyde British on the demise of their overlord. The death of Adils (as with the death of Thorir Longchin at Hafrsfjord) leads to the end of the obligation to fight. The professionalism of Thorolf's unit allows it to conduct a fighting withdrawal.

The final act of Brunanburh for the saga writer is the confrontation between Egil and King Athelstan. In the story, the Saxon king represents the principle which sacrifices all for power. The clan of Kveldulf was divided into two characteristic types of dark and fair Maera-men. Thorolf, as a representative of the latter type, was susceptible to the glamour surrounding royalty. Egil, one of the dark Maera-men,

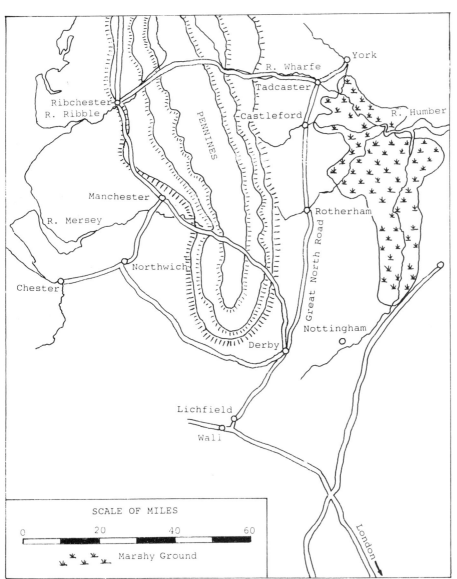

The precise location of the battlefield of Brunanburh has never been determined, but it almost certainly lies within the area of this map. Most of the evidence points to a site on the Great North Road to the east of the Pennines somewhere between Derby and Rotherham.

▶*Hacksilver, coins and ingots from the Cuerdale hoard, possibly the paychest of a Viking Army. The change from plunder to regular payment in such silver 'monetary specie' brought one of the greatest differences in the character of the Viking warrior towards the end of the Viking period. (By courtesy of the Board of Trustees, British Museum).*

23

retained the scepticism of an earlier independent age. Thorolf's trust had brought him to his death and Egil now sought redress for the loss to his clan.

After an effective and bloody pursuit Egil returned to bury his brother on the battlefield with due solemnity and two poems, one on the glory of Thorolf and the sorrow occasioned by his death and another on Egil's personal triumphs. Duty fulfilled, the surviving brother returned to the king's headquarters, where a celebratory feast was under way. According to the saga Athelstan made arrangements for Egil to be seated in a place of honour but this was clearly insufficient to the son of Skallagrim who sat fully equipped and scowling. Eventually when the king restored the balance of respect and recognition by passing to the bereaved warrior a gold arm-ring (symbolically presented on the point of a sword) Egil felt able to take off his armour and join the festivities

Maldon 991

The greatest Old English battle poem is an untitled piece on the death of Byhrtnoth, the Ealdorman of Essex. Not only is this the major source for the events of the Battle of Maldon but it also provides the clearest statement of the Germanic Heroic Ideal. Historically the battle sealed the fate of the Saxon kingdom and began a train of events which was to lead to the destruction of the Wessex dynasty.

By the end of the 10th century the Scandinavian invaders had not won a battle in England for over hundred years. The independence of the Danelaw had been eroded in a series of devasting campaigns and a network of *burhs* was established to maintain centralised control. Attempts by a joint Viking army to break the Saxon position in Essex had centred on siege of the fortification at Maldon in 925. The arrival of a relief force had prevented the fall of the town and the front line of the Saxon resurgence moved further north to the Kingdom of York, where Norse penetr

The site of the battle of Maldon showing the extensive areas of salt flats and marsh which restricted where combat could take place. The Norsemen were camped on Northey Island in the centre of the map and the causeway inevitably became the focus of the initial struggle. After the Saxons withdrew, the bulk of the fighting took place on the solid ground south-west of the causeway.

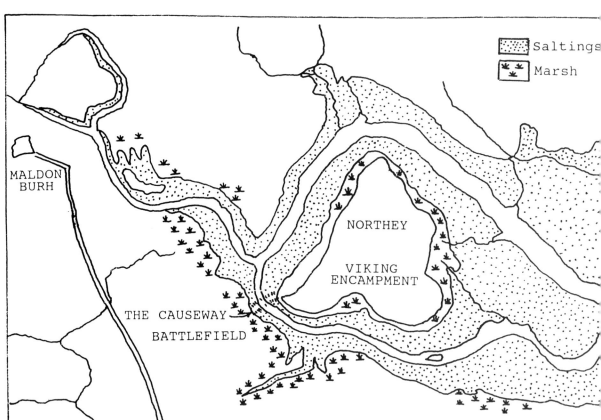

◄Sword with heavily corroded blade on which are traces of the remnants of a scabbard. The scabbard has coalesced with the blade as each deteriorated. Viking-age scabbards are rarely found in better condition than this. (By courtesy of the Board of Trustees, British Museum)

▲Broken sword of Petersen type T. A slight twist in the blade (barely visible in this photo) suggests that it was broken as part of a ritual. (By courtesy of the Board of Trustees, British Museum)

ation had been more complete. By the year of the second Battle of Maldon the Saxon domination of the lowland zone of Britain was total. The kingdom had been divided into areas of subordinate authority each controlled by an Ealdorman. These were unlike the minor kings of the earlier period with a personal connection to their region, but were royal officials who could be appointed, dismissed or transferred. One of these was Byhrtnoth, a man of noble family who was initially the ealdorman of East Anglia but subsequently moved to the less important posting of Essex in his advanced age.

In the 980s Viking raiders again appeared off the coast of England. These were not led by the minor chieftains of a displaced Norwegian nobility or land-hungry farmers from overcrowded Scandinavia. They were a mixed band of freebooters seeking immediate and large gains in silver. The exhaustion of the Central Asian silver mines had lead to the collapse of the Russian trade routes and the necessity to introduce a new source of wealth to Viking spheres of influence. Interestingly the leaders of the new wave of Viking attacks included men like Thorkell the Tall (one of the captains of the semi-professional Jomsvikings) and Olaf Tryggvason (the pretender to the throne of Norway), both men who needed money to further their ambitions at home.

The revived raids on eastern England in the summer of 991 differed from the small scale of affairs of previous decades. Major cities, like Ipswich, now became viable targets for large raiding armies. The Vikings at Maldon were said to have deployed a fleet of 93 ships, although the exact size of the invading

Petersen's Typology of Spears (left to right): A: leaf bladed with short socket; B: leaf bladed with short winged socket; C: leaf bladed with long winged socket; D: short angular profile with long winged socket; E: long, narrow, leaf-bladed type with long socket; F: Angular blade, with strickening (shallow curving) above the angle, and long socket.

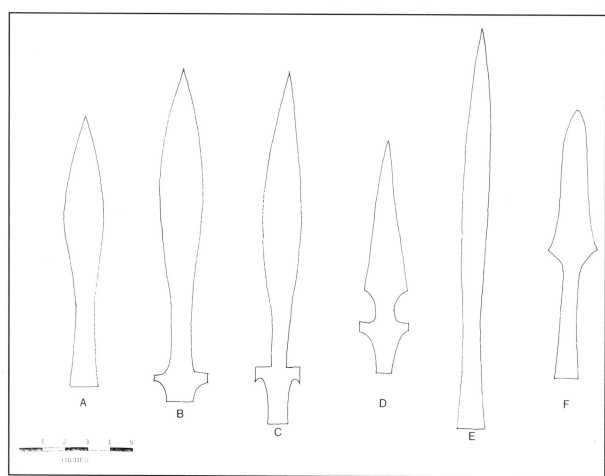

A   B   C   D   E   F

1 2 3 1 5
INCHES

army cannot be inferred from this as the number of men in a ship's crew is not known. The estimates are in the region of several thousand warriors.

The defending forces under Byhrtnoth included his own personal bodyguard, probably a fairly large unit as the Ealdorman's career had been long and successful and his popularity sufficient to persuade men to fight on after the normal bonds of agreement demanded. The local levy or fyrd was also present in large numbers. Maldon was a local centre of sufficient importance to house a royal mint and the area of Essex would have been mobilised by the threat of the Vikings. The training and morale of the fyrd was of variable quality but generally low. This lack of expertise and dedication was to prove disastrous.

After plundering Ipswich, the Vikings rounded the Tendring peninsula and entered the estuary of the Blackwater. They established themselves on the Island of Northey, in the time-honoured manner of Vikings on a hostile coast, and although the *burh* at Maldon appears to have defied or missed their attentions they were firmly in position when Byhrtnoth arrived to take up position on the landward side of Northey's tidal causeway.

That both protagonists were eager to give battle would perhaps indicate an equality of forces. Byhrtnoth's motivations in bringing the pirates to battle may have included a desire to prevent them escaping to ravage other areas or even a genuine belief that the forces facing him could be defeated by his own command. The poem makes it clear that the Ealdorman was in full and effective control of his force from the start, when he gives instructions to his noble followers to release their hawks and drive away their horses. The poet appears to be saying that beasts were free to depart the place of slaughter but that men, bound by honour and obligation, must remain.

The defence of the causeway

Within the poem of the battle we are given a literary interpretation of the course of an early medieval engagement. A messenger from the Viking host brings Byhrtnoth a demand from his leaders which can be summarised as a demand for money with menaces. The Ealdorman hotly rejects this in an answer which forges the ideas of loyalty (in this case to King Ethelred), national pride and a personal refusal to be intimidated into a response that invites the Norsemen to do their worst. Having rejected blackmail, Byhrtnoth now commits his forces to a desperate engagement which resolves itself into three sections. The first is an exchange of missiles across the tidal creek which separates Northey from the mainland, developing into a defence of the causeway access by three champions. The literal truth of all this might be difficult to prove and it should be borne in mind that the poet was probably influenced by the classical story of 'Horatius on the Bridge'. Attempts to rationalise this phase of the poem's narrative have included the interpretation of the three Saxon heroes as the commanders of sub-units detailed to an important post.

Failing to break the Saxon position on the narrow land-bridge the 'heathens' again send a messenger who asks that the battle should be continued on the mainland. In agreeing to this request Byhrtnoth opens himself to accusations by the poet of being overly courageous (though the word *ofermod* may not imply foolhardiness). Like the Battle of Brunanburh the fight at Maldon might have been governed by

conventions only dimly understood today. The Ealdorman's wish to force a conclusion led to the 'pagans' being allowed to cross to a more convenient site on the land and the continuation of the struggle. As the English came under increasing pressure they began to lose heart and Byhrtnoth's mistake in putting his horse in the charge of one Godric, proved disastrous when Godric mounted and fled. The levy of Essex mistook Godric for the Ealdorman himself, and behaved accordingly.

The isolated bodyguard was now at the mercy of the Vikings, and again we see the tactics of an all-out attack on the supreme commander. Byhrtnoth is struck by a thrown javelin. In death Byhrtnoth's thoughts were on refuge with a Christian God as much as glory. His household troop resolved to end

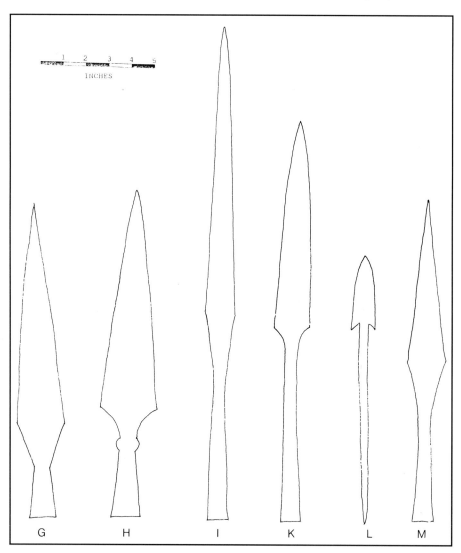

Spear typology (left to right): G: broad angular blade with short socket; H: broad angular blade with medium-length socket; I: long, narrow, angular blade with long socket; K: medium-length, narrow, angular blade with long socket; L: barbed javelin head with long tang; M: medium-length angular blade with medium-length socket.

ighting around the body of their lord. (The laws of he Jomsvikings included a similar refusal to give ground, but allowed for retreat if faced by overwhelming odds.)

The subsequent action of King Ethelred in paying ever-increasing sums of Danegeld to Scandinavian invaders was as much a response to the entire late 10th century wave of attacks as the single defeat of Maldon. The payments were to fund the national invasions of the early 11th century under the Danish kings. The Anglo-Norse elite which emerged from this period based much of its military power on a version of the household warrior bands typified by the Royal Huscarls of Harold Godwinson who were to fight and die at Hastings.

MOTIVATION AND PSYCHOLOGY

The earliest references to the warrior ideals of the Germanic races can be found in the work of classical authors from Strabo onwards. The sacrifice of the fruits of victory by ritual destruction is to be seen in Danish bog deposits of the Iron Age and is described in the *Universal History* of Orosius. Sacrifice is recognised as the fulfilment of specific vows, something the Graeco-Roman world was perfectly familiar with. Captured wealth, equipment and prisoners were dedicated to the gods in return for assistance in winning battles. The conviction that the battlefield was the province of a powerful warrior deity survived among the Nordic people long after the conversion to Christianity of the more southerly Germanic tribes of the continent.

The name of the Scandinavian battle-god is not always the same, being concealed by euphemisms and metaphorical titles. At least two alternative war-gods existed as detailed by the Icelandic writer Snorri Sturluson. These were Tyr, a specialised battle-god, and Odin, the father of the gods and a more complex figure whose areas of interest extended to all aspects of power politics.

Violence as a way of life remained part of the

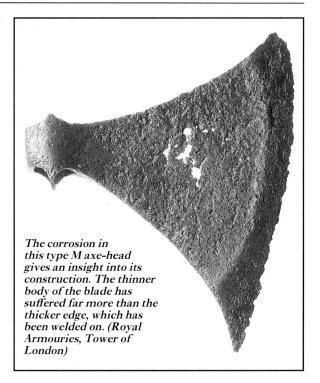

The corrosion in this type M axe-head gives an insight into its construction. The thinner body of the blade has suffered far more than the thicker edge, which has been welded on. (Royal Armouries, Tower of London)

Scandinavian ethos until well into the Middle Ages, when Christianity was long established. It is not possible to explain away the whole of Scandinavian warfare by references to the battle-gods. In many ways the god was a symptom of a violent culture rather than the cause of it.

If Sturluson's account can be believed, the Viking warrior found his fitting home in the Hall of Odin, Valhalla. Here Odin presided over the ultimate expression of the gift economy, providing the chosen with all that was good on an unbelievably lavish scale and the benefit of fighting to the death with daily resurrections. Odin's recruitment of warriors might be justified in early medieval pagan terms by the argument that the larger the warband the more powerful the leader. The motive given by Sturluson has further implications. Odin is raising an army of super-warriors to fight at the apocalyptic battle of Ragnarok. This sounds suspiciously like the later medieval interpretation of the place of the human soul in heaven. The Christian God is recruiting perfected souls to replace the fallen angels. However, Sturluson was a Christian writing for a Christian audience. It is not even certain that the average Viking even believed in Sturluson's version of Valhalla. The extent to which his descriptions of Norse religion reflect reality can never now be fully assessed as no pagan version of the Norse myths survives for comparison.

The conceptual cosmos of the Viking warrior might be bounded at the supernatural level by a final fight alongside a generous and worthy lord. The earthly world was governed by essentially the same concept. The lord in early Germanic society was a crucial figure around whom society revolved. The origin of the word in the Old English *Hlaf-ord* (Loaf ward), the controller of bread, gives us a clue to this central position. In a primitive farming community the man who dominated the distribution of food was the effective ruler. It was this idea of a ruling figure which was to evolve first into an extended local lordship and finally into the monarchy. As the nature of power changed, the attitudes of the warrior changed with them.

The nature of leadership

Ganga Hrolf, a son of Jarl Rognvald of Moer, found himself exiled from Norway for breaking the ban on raiding within Harald Harfargi's realm. Ganga and his followers operated along the Seine in the early part of the 10th century and ultimately dominated it to such an extent that the Frankish monarchy was forced to cede the future duchy of Normandy to them. During the negotiations with the Franks an often quoted exchange occurred as recorded by Dudo of St. Quentin. When questioned as to the authority of their leader they replied that he had no authority as all were equal. This may be simply an evasive answer but we know from the later history of the duchy that Rolf or Rollo was in fact the leader of this group. The nature of leadership amongst the earlier raiding parties is somewhat unclear. The bands of Vikings operating in north-western Europe between the end of the 8th century and the end of the 10th century appear to have joined together or separated as circumstance required.

Long-term commitment did not extend beyond the immediate leader of a warrior's group, who might very probably be a native of one's own region if not a near relative. This form of close-knit group gains certain obvious advantages. Unity of purpose is liable to be stronger. In battle the unit will act in a more cohesive and mutually supportive way, and the abandoning of wounded comrades is less likely.

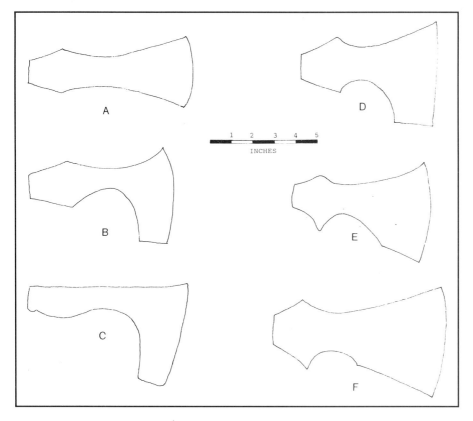

Petersen's Typology of Axes (top to bottom): A: symmetrical profile with shallow curve to tips of the edge; B: asymmetrical profile with deep, sharp curve to lower side and 'bearded' edge; C: asymmetrical with level top side, deep sharp curve to lower side and bearded edge; D: asymmetrical with deep, slow curve to lower side, shallow curve to lower side and bearded edge; E: asymmetrical with shallow, slow curve and straight extension along lower side to meet bearded edge, and shallow curve to top side; F: asymmetrical with shallow curve to top side, short shallow curve along lower side and long straight extension to meet bearded edge.

Good commanders commonly toured their armies immediately prior to battle to make sure that all was ready for action. Encouraging speeches were made to strengthen the resolve of the combatants and sometimes poetry was composed on the spot. This showed not only the sophistication of the poet but also his composure, a quality that would hopefully be transmitted to his followers.

Extreme behaviour during battle was commonplace. Such actions might be based in a religion that glorified the warrior and made the prerequisite for a suitable after-life the display of superlative fighting qualities. Sagas abound with desperate engagements where the main motivation of the participant is not mere survival. A man who faced odds was testing his own worth, and at the same time, his luck against his enemies.

Strength of purpose was another Viking trait. While Erik Bloodaxe was enjoying his brief and unpopular reign in Norway, Egil Skallagrimson had fallen foul of Queen Gunnhilda. The king had ordered Egil's death, but the Icelander had shown himself too elusive for the tyrant. Trapped on an island by the royal retainers who were carefully guarding all boats, Egil stripped his equipment. Making a bundle of his sword, helmet and spear (less the shaft, discarded to create a handier weapon) he swam to a nearby islet. As the search for him widened, a small boat with 12 fighting men landed on his refuge where he was keeping careful watch. Nine of the party went inland and Egil attacked the remainder making use of the local terrain and a sudden assault. Cutting down one man in the first onset he sliced the foot from a second who tried to flee up a slope. The survivor was attempting to pole off the boat when Egil seized a trailing rope and hauled his prey in. No single Norwegian was ever a match for Egil at the height of his strength and the victim was soon despatched. The implication is clear, two of Egil's opponents were killed because their nerve had failed them. Egil, however, had maintained his presence of mind and with tremendous strength of purpose evaded the might of King Erik.

The kind of resolve and immediate action which characterised Egil's behaviour is consistently held up in Norse literature as the role model for the warrior. The *Havamal*, the mythical advice of Odin to mankind, contains a series of verses stressing the virtue of careful consideration and attack. This theme, in its oral form, was one of the major influences on the mind of the Viking *hersir*.

APPEARANCE AND EQUIPMENT

The earliest large-scale seaborne raid of Scandinavians on Europe was that conducted by the Geats under Hygelac. The leaders of this southern Swedish tribe can be expected to have carried equipment comparable to that found in the elite status graves of Valsgarde and Vendel. The panoplies yielded by these sites are similar to those discovered at Sutton Hoo in Suffolk. The Valsgarde garniture included a set of armour far more extensive than any we have evidence for in the Viking period proper. By the end of the 8th century the splinted limb armour of the Valsgarde chieftain appears to have fallen out of use. Arguments have been made for the re-emergence of such items in the Byzantine-influenced armour of the Varangian Guard. However equipment such as this can never have been widespread and was probably of little value in mobile warfare. The warriors who descended on Lindisfarne in 793 were almost certain-

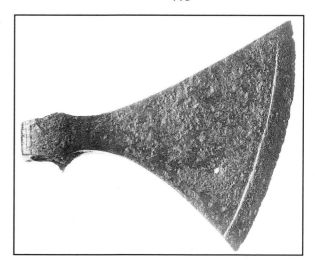

This type L axe-head shows similarities with the type M into which it develops, including the shape of the blade, which curves downwards and inwards to allow for an overhead blow. (Royal Armouries, Tower of London)

ly less well fitted out. Even the war-gear of a local leader would not have been so complete as that of his 7th-century predecessor. This reduction of armament would appear to correspond to a change in the nature of war as practised by the Vikings. Territorial battles in the homelands were no longer the only profitable outlet for Scandinavian energies. More mobile forms of war would require the warrior to be more lightly equipped.

Clothing and grooming

Observers in the early Middle Ages comment on the great care Norsemen took over their general appearance. The number of combs found on Viking sites show a deep concern for grooming. The well-coiffured head on the Sigtuna elk-antler carving, with its impressive handlebar moustache, show this to be more than just an interest in de-lousing. Personal hygiene 'kits', some highly decorative, have been found in both male and female graves. These include tweezers for plucking superfluous hair and tiny spoons for removing ear-wax. Only a person of status could afford to spend time on such activities. Consequently a well turned out appearance would be the hallmark of the warrior of middle or high rank.

Dressing for war was not so much a matter of uniform or camouflage but an expression of wealth and pride. The warrior would appear in his finest and most conspicuous clothing. In *Njal's Saga*, Skarp-Hedin dresses before violent encounters in the most ostentatious fashion. Participants in feuds are recognised at distance by characteristic items of apparel. The intention often appears to be the advertisement rather than concealment of their presence.

Shoes and boots were constructed of leather or hide usually obtained from cattle but sometimes from seals or reindeer. The ancient name for a hide shoe was *Hriflingr*. The *hersir* might be expected to wear more elegant footwear of dressed skin like those found in Hungate and Coppergate in York. Boots and shoes were made in a variety of styles. They could be cut from a single piece of leather or made up from two sections stitched along a vamp—a seam running along the upper towards the toe of the shoe. Soles were usually made from separate pieces of leather. Footwear could be in other than natural colours. Skarp-Hedin for example, had a black pair. A sock was discovered at Coppergate knitted of woollen yarn, but apparently not shaped to allow for the heel and toes.

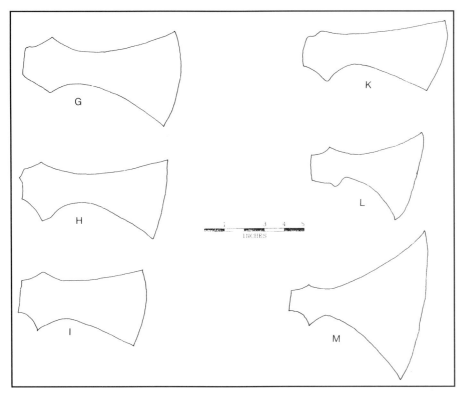

Axe typology (top to bottom): G: symmetrical profile with extension horns to blade; H: asymmetrical with long shallow curve along lower side; I: asymmetrical with long shallow curve along lower side, broad across the body of the blade; K: asymmetrical with slight curve to upper side and long shallow curve to lower side; L: asymmetrical with long shallow curve to upper horn and shorter steep curve to lower horn; M: asymmetrical with long steep curve to upper horn and shorter steep curve to lower horn.

1: Scandinavian warrior, 6th-7th Centuries
2: Detail of helmet construction

1

2

A

The Battlefield of Hafrsfjord c.872

B

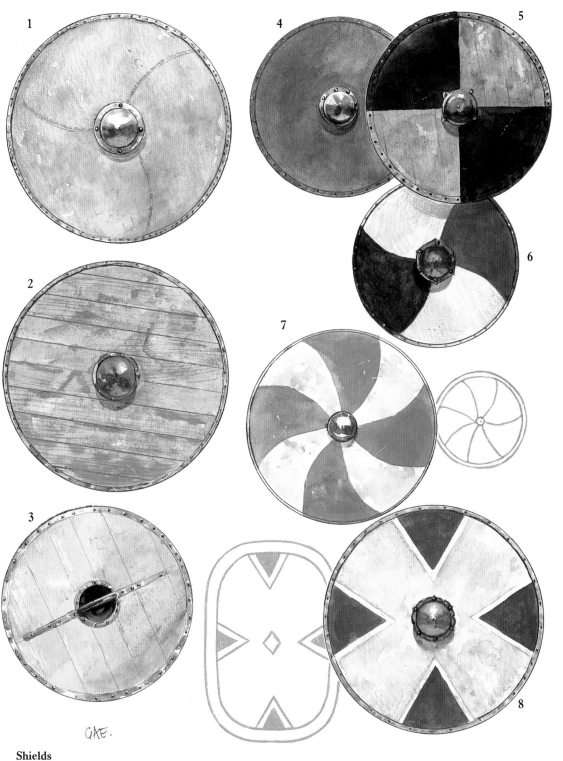

GAE.

Shields

1: Leather faced shield

2: Gokstad, late 9th C.

3: Shield with ferrous rim, early 10th C.

4: Red war shield, late 10th C.

5, 6, 7: Typical shield patterns

8: From Oseberg tapestry

Training: the *skjaldborg* (shield wall)

D

The Battle of Brunanburh

E

1: Viking warrior, 8th-9th Centuries
2: Spear construction

Weaponsmith's workshop

Swords and axes
1: Fyrkat, 10th C.
2: Decorated axe, Botnhamm
3: Broad bladed axe, 10th-11th C.
4: 'Bearded' axe
5: Jutland, 11th C.
6: Decorated axe, Mammen
7, 8: Sword typology
9: The Sword of Ireland, 9th C.
10. Hedeby, 10th-11th C.
11: Type X

12: Blade signed by maker
13: Ireland, Lough Derg, c.1100
14: Dybäck, 10th C.
15: Temple church, 10th C.

H

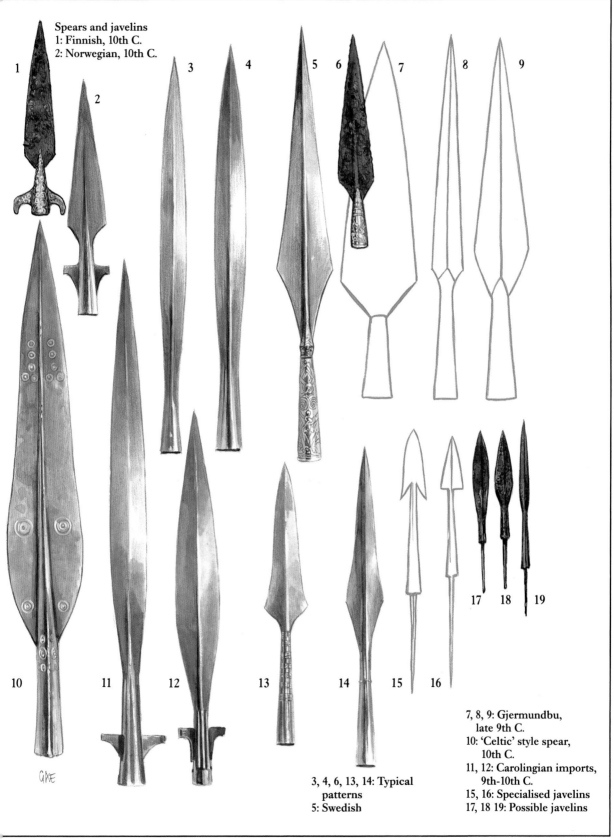

Spears and javelins
1: Finnish, 10th C.
2: Norwegian, 10th C.

3, 4, 6, 13, 14: Typical
     patterns
5: Swedish

7, 8, 9: Gjermundbu,
    late 9th C.
10: 'Celtic' style spear,
    10th C.
11, 12: Carolingian imports,
    9th-10th C.
15, 16: Specialised javelins
17, 18 19: Possible javelins

I

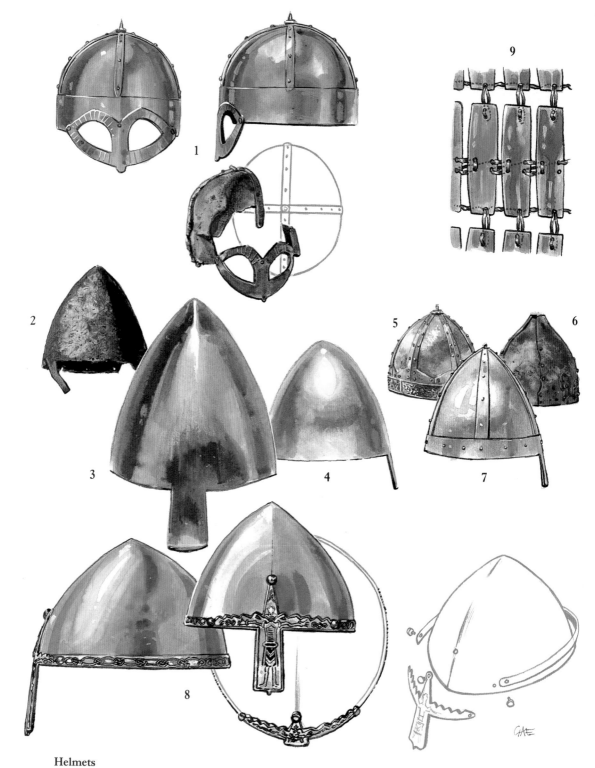

Helmets
1: Gjermundbu, late 9th C.
2: Olmütz
3: Poznań, 11th C.

4: Hainburg
5: Chalons-sur-Saône, 6th C.
6: Giecz, 11th C.

7: Typical pattern, 11th C.
8: Wenceslas, 11th C.
9: Lacing of Birka armour

J

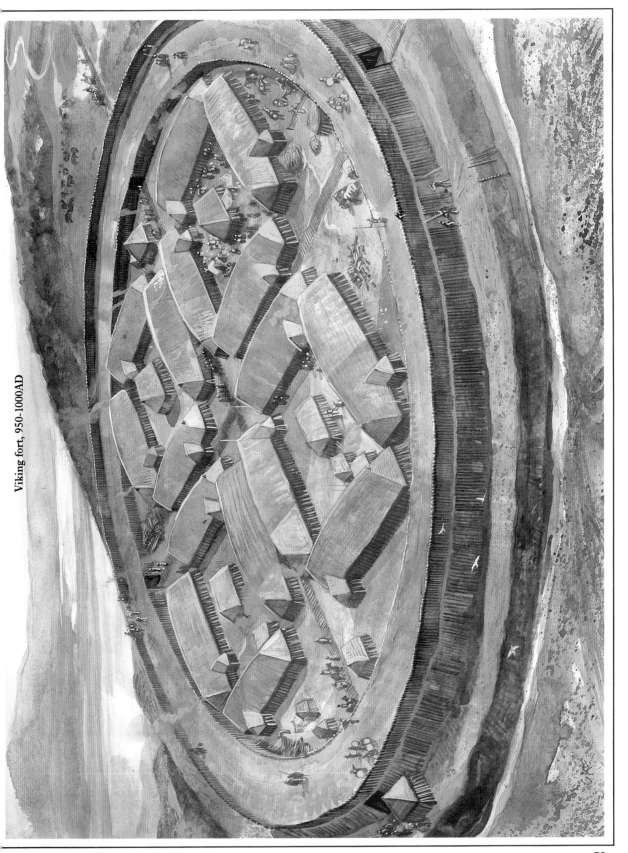

Viking fort, 950-1000AD

K

1: Later Viking warrior, 10th-11th C.
2: Construction of sword hilt

2

1

After the 11th century, swords of type X (as on the right) were supplanted by fullered broadswords with more varied designs (such as the two examples on the left and centre). (Royal Armouries, Tower of London)

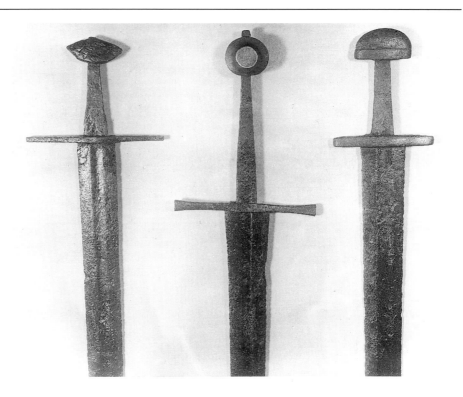

Trousers of varying fullness were worn in the 7th to 9th centuries. The Gotland gravestones and the tapestries from Skogg and Oseberg show them as baggy and gathered anywhere from mid-calf to just below the knee. The Gotland gravestones show clearly that they were worn in combat. The Oseberg tapestry depicts the same full trousers as the dress of the high-status warrior. Tight-fitting trousers became more fashionable in the 10th and 11th centuries. This may be due to Scandinavian exposure to English and continental fashion. By the early 11th century King Cnut is shown wearing close-fitting hose or stockings. These seem to be bound around the mid-leg with strips or garters of decorated material below which the fitting appears to be somewhat wrinkled. Trousers were made either of linen or woven wool. Other constructional details are lost as the various contemporary depictions do not show seams.

Tunics

Representations of tunics from the first two centuries of the Viking Age show knee-length garments with full skirts gathered at the waist, usually by a belt. There is little change until the later part of the period. The neck of the tunic could be square or round, and was fastened by a drawstring, garment hook, or sometimes by a single bead used as a button. The sleeves were usually long, to the wrist or longer. From the elbow to the cuff the sleeve was close-fitting but not tight enough to prevent wrinkles appearing when pushed back up the fore-arm. A placket might be fitted around the neckhole or a length of tablet-woven braid. Similar decoration might be found applied to the hem and cuffs. Embroidery was an alternative to braid. Sections of material of a contrasting colour could be inset to add width to the skirt of the tunic.

The colours used on the Bayeux Tapestry are a good guide to those available in the Viking period. Dyeing technology is not likely to have changed radically before the end of the 11th century. The impressive permanence of the Bayeux colours suggests the use of an effective (and presumably expensive) mordant. There is no reason that such materials would not have been available in Scandinavia by import, if not by indigenous production. Undyed material was probably widely used by the poor, although Vikings of higher status would favour more colourful attire.

Cloaks of rectangular or square shape appear to have been the norm, they can be seen worn by warriors though not usually in combat. They were held at the shoulders by a brooch or pin. Embroidered cloaks are also mentioned in the sagas. Hoods could be improvised by folding the cloaks or possibly added to the garment as separate pieces of material.

Relics of civilian headgear, which would have been worn when helmets were inappropriate, include the fur-trimmed hat from Birka which was influenced by eastern fashions. The detached hood of red-brown tabby-weave silk found in the Coppergate dig is assumed to be an item of female dress, although the main argument for this appears to be a photograph of the item being worn by a rather fetching 20th century lady researcher. Hats of felt are described in several sagas and Odin is said to have worn a broad-brimmed version as part of a disguise.

Other dress accessories (which might also be worn in battle), include leather belts with decorated buckles and strap ends. Belts were usually narrow, less than one inch wide. Belt fittings were mostly of copper alloy, examples carved in bone and painted in verdigris were less common. Additional equipment could include a leather pouch, Purses were often of the type cut as a thin disc of leather closed by a drawstring looped through holes in the rim. A larger version of this, the *nestbaggin*, acted as a haversack for the campaigning *Hersir*.

Helmets

The only helmet that can be definitely ascribed to the Vikings is one found at Gjermundbu, and is usually dated to the later 9th century. In outward appearance it follows the earlier tradition of Scandinavian helmets having a fixed visor of the characteristic 'spectacle' form. However, there are considerable differences in structure. The Gjermundbu helmet is formed by a brow band, a skeleton of two metal bars and four shaped plates which make up the dome. One of the bars is aligned along the centre of the skull and the other across the bowl from ear to ear. Both bars are attached to the brow band as is the fixed visor. The four sections of the dome are rivetted to the cross pieces to fill the spaces between the various components. The pre-Viking Valsgarde and Vendel helmets are altogether more elaborate. Some of them have an additional reinforcing crest or *wala*, others cheek pieces. The helmets of the true Viking age have more in common with the Gjermundbu specimen.

A carved elk-antler from Sigtuna in Sweden, depicts a warrior wearing a conical helmet. This appears to be of four shaped plates held together by rivets. Although it shows no sign of any structural members, a row of rivets around the base of the helmet indicates the presence of at least a brow band.

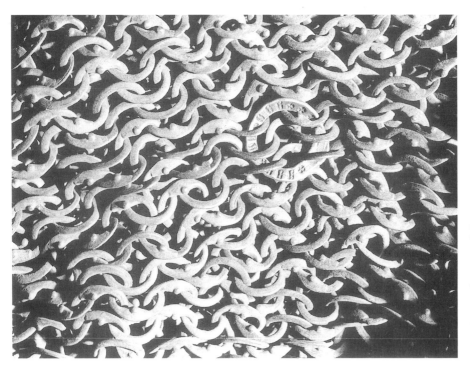

Although from considerably later than the Viking period, this section of mail shirt is a good example of the riveting and linking of the rings. The oversize ring in the centre is the maker's signature ring and is made of copper alloy. (Royal Armouries, Tower of London)

Worked from a single piece of metal the Olmütz helmet is probably the product of a Central European workshop. The helmet was held in the treasury of Olmütz

Monastery until it was transferred to the Waffensammlung in Vienna where it is today. (Kunsthistorisches Museum, Vienna)

This rear view of the Olmütz helmet clearly shows the ridge running from front to back and the rivet holes for the lining's brow band. The evidence for the use of this type of

helmet by later Norse warriors is based on gravestone carvings and the Bayeux Tapestry. (Kunsthistorisches Museum, Vienna)

A nasal extension shown on this piece might be interpreted as a projection of the longitudinal skull band, though this is not certain.

Viking monumental art, for example the Kirlevington, Sockburn and Middleton cross fragments, show figures wearing what are probably conical helmets but could equally be pointed caps or hoods. The Weston Church cross fragment shows a bareheaded warrior.

Two famous helmets from Central Europe commonly associated with the Viking period are the 'Olmutz' helmet, displayed in Vienna, and the 'St. Wenceslas' helmet from the Treasury of Prague Cathedral. The dome of each is a one-piece forging. While there is no evidence that this technique was used by Norse armourers, the dating of these items and the diverse nature of the equipment used by the Vikings suggests helmets of this type may have been in use. Olaf the Saint is said to have deployed a unit of 100 picked men at the Battle of Nesjar armed in coats of mail and 'foreign' helmets.

Armour

No complete hauberk of mail survives from the period and even fragments are rare. Mail retained its value as a form of defence until after the Middle Ages and would have been reused by succeeding generations. But this alone does not explain the paucity of finds. The level of usage among the Vikings may have been quite low. The poetry found within sagas, usually taken to be of much earlier date than the main body of text, frequently refers to byrnies. Mention of mail armour becomes more common when later events are described, perhaps implying more frequent use. The inference of Sturluson's *Heimskringla* is that by the Battle of Stamford Bridge (1066) the Norwegian army's lack of mail contributed to its defeat. The Norwegians had in fact left their armour aboard their ships at Riccall. The verses made up in the course of the battle by Harald Hardrada refer to the deficiency. The King himself had a mail-shirt considered important enough to have a name— '*Emma*', described as being unusually long at knee-length. Mail probably became more common and covered more of the body as the period progressed. The continental fashion for mail coifs might also have been followed by the Vikings. The Huscarls of the late Saxon kingdom were, racially, of Danish origin. The Bayeux Tapestry indicates a similarity of gear between the Saxons and Normans; and the Normans certainly appear to be wearing coifs.

There exists a little evidence that lamellar armour was used in Scandinavia. Such armour is generally thought to be of Eastern origin. A few plates were found at Birka, now an isolated farm but once one of the major trading towns of central Sweden. The eastern connections of this merchant settlement may explain the presence of this unusual find.

There is also little evidence for the use of leather or fabric armour. Sturluson, in the *Heimskringla*, mentions the gift of 13 body armours of reindeer hide to King Olaf the Saint. These were said to be more resistant to attack than mail hauberks. What may be quilted jacks of layered fabric armour appear on the Gotland tombstones. But this is uncertain because of the nature of this type of art.

Shields

The Gotland gravestones show warriors with what appear to be bucklers. The proportions of the figures which carry them suggest they were 24 inches or less in diameter. Such items may have been in use but no archaeological evidence survives to confirm this. Had the sculptor of the Gotland gravestones attempted to depict a shield of three feet in diameter this would have produced a large blank expanse on the figure. The artist may have sacrificed strict proportions for the sake of producing a more detailed human subject. Other examples of this disregard for proportions so typical of the art of the period can be seen on the Gotland stones.

The largest group of surviving shields from the Viking Age was part of the ship burial at Gokstad. However, these shields may have been made specially for the burial and could be unrepresentative of those used in combat. Experiments, carried out in 1990 by Daniel Ezra of City University revealed that a reproduction Gokstad shield was unwieldly in individual combat and tiring to use in close formation. Shield bosses have been relatively common finds. It has been assumed that many shields had metal rims;

in fact not a single excavated shield has been found with a complete metal rim. Organic components of shields are usually decayed to a point which defied early excavation techniques.

In the first centuries of the Viking period shields appear to have always been circular. The curious oval shield which appears in the Oseberg tapestry has no parallel from archaeology. The kite-shaped shields, which were first beginning to appear in Scandinavia during the 11th century, were called *Holfinn-skjoldr*. The extent to which these were used in the late Viking Age is difficult to estimate, but Anglo-Norse Huscarls appear to have been almost exclusively equipped with them by the Battle of Hastings. Such highly paid professional military retainers might be expected to have followed the latest continental fashion.

Although shield blazons are often ascribed to Viking warriors in the much later Icelandic sagas, such evidence is of limited value. Such descriptions are usually thought to refer to medieval practices. Two characters in *Brennu-Njals* Saga are said to have had shields decorated with a dragon and a lion respectively. This may be anachronistic, but it is only necessary to consider the various animal representations on Bayeux Tapestry shields to recognise that they may have been in use less than a century earlier.

Symbolic shields were employed by Greenlanders in the Vinland expeditions, red to indicate warlike intentions and white for peace. The followers of Olaf the Saint are reputed to have carried white shields with a gilt, red or blue cross in 1015. This design was influenced by the aggressive Christianity of their leader but also served to distinguish them from their pagan opponents in battle.

WEAPONS

The typical offensive weapons found at Viking sites are the sword, axe, spear and bow. The majority of such sites are graves. Danish deposits of the early period include the same range of weapons as Swedish and Norwegian sites; but the early adoption of Christianity in Denmark brought an end to the custom of burying a warrior with his weapons and this has reduced the sample of later Danish finds.

Swords

The commonest form of Viking sword (of which over 2,000 have been found in Scandinavia alone) is the long, straight, two-edged type. These were usually about three feet long with a simple cross-guard and some form of pommel. The blade was generally fullered for lightness and strength. The points of such swords were comparatively blunt as they were intended more for cutting than stabbing. Such weapons could be purely functional or highly decorative. Fittings of copper alloy were more common in Scandinavia than in Europe, but even so pommels and cross guards of ferrous metal were the norm. When not in use the sword was carried in a scabbard of wood, usually covered in leather with a metal chape. The interior of the scabbard was ideally lined with sheepskin, the wool side inwards, the natural greases protecting the metal of the blade. Scabbards were usually suspended from a waist belt but could be worn over the shoulder on a baldric.

An important local variant of the longsword was the three-foot, single-edged version sometimes called the long-sax. This type is generally Norwegian in origin and has a single edge like the true sax commonly associated with the Saxons. Long-saxes are found with fittings that are roughly similar to those on swords. The majority of blades in this group appear to be made by pattern-welding techniques which probably indicates they were high status items.

Single-edged knives of more modest proportions are frequently found at Viking sites. Their enormous numbers (around 300 in the Coppergate dig of 1976–81 alone) argue for their use in everyday life as

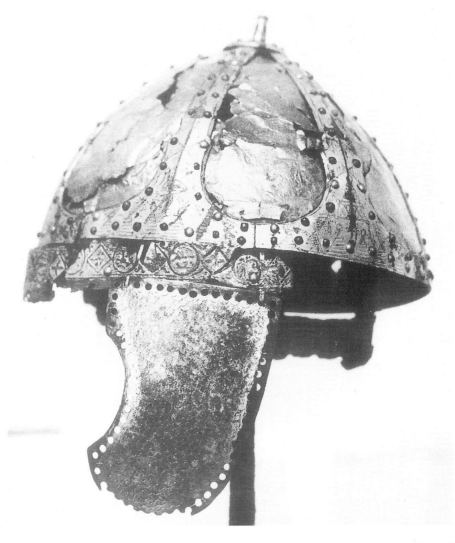

The Spangenhelm, originally based on Central Asian styles, continued to influence European helmets as late as the 'Great Polish' series of the 11th century. This particular example, with a frame of six uprights, is later 5th or early 6th century. (Kunsthistorisches Museum, Vienna)

This later form of Spangenhelm with four plates is probably from the 6th century, but is similar in design to the 'Great Polish' series. (Kunsthistorisches Museum, Vienna)

eating implements and tools. The somewhat larger saxes also encountered, may have been hunting weapons rather than military arms. The level of decorative inlay on saxes of this type certainly points to their use by the wealthy.

Axes

Axes of the period are also decorated according to the owner's status The splendid Mammen axe without its inlaid silver design would be no more than a common wood-chopping tool. The shape of axe-heads differed according to purpose, although it should be noted that a wood-axe might make a serviceable weapon. The broad-bladed axes wielded with two hands, which appear in the latter part of the period, are specialised items. By the time of Hastings they were almost the distinguishing mark of Anglo-Danish Huscarls and may have been a response to the increased use of mail. Axes with 'beards' or downward extensions to the blade have sometimes been identified as specifically Nordic. Given the widespread appearance of similar styles in the Middle Ages this is far from certain.

Staff weapons other than spears make no appearance in the Viking archaeological record. Perhaps funerary custom ignored the halberds and bills described in sagas or these are later intrusions into Old Norse literature. The curious mail-piercer described as part of Egil Skallagrimson's equipment at Brunanburh sounds like a glaive, a development of the agricultural bill-hook with additional prongs for use in combat. Such weapons are known from Merovingian Frankish graves and are often seen in illustrations post-dating the Vikings, but most examples are actually later medieval. The type does not seem to have been much used by Scandinavians of the 8th to the 11th centuries.

Spears

An early survey of Danish graves revealed that the spear was only the third most frequent weapon deposited after axe and sword. The value of the spear in fighting and hunting argues for a more widespread use than this evidence indicates. Since spearheads were cheaper and quicker to manufacture than the other favoured weapons of the period, it seems likely that spears were more usually carried than swords. The very cheapness of spears might account for their being used less often as grave goods.

Many of the spears associated with the Vikings are Carolingian imports identified by a characteristic broad blade and wings projecting from the socket. The latter feature is analogous to the cross-pieces on later boar-spears which prevent the shaft penetrating too deep into the victim. Modern experiment shows they could also be used to hook an opponent's shield aside. Spears with narrower blades may be interpreted as javelins, although a dual purpose is implied in literary sources. The intricate decoration sometimes found on this type of spear does not rule out their use as throwing weapons. The thrower might reasonably expect to recover his spear afterwards. Personalised decoration would allow instant recognition and the thrower's skill would be undeniably shown when his weapon was extracted from a defeated foe.

MANUFACTURE OF WEAPONS

Accounts of Viking weapons manufacture, mostly contained in Icelandic sources, tend to concentrate on the more exalted heirlooms or even magical arms of heroes. The descriptions are often obscured by formulae of mystical significance. It is impossible to say how accurate these accounts might be, but a certain level of ceremony was probably expected in the creation of a special weapon. It may be that these curious descriptions of forging techniques are simply misunderstandings of the complexities of the smith's craft. The difficulties of attempting to use sagas as historical accounts are clearly demonstrated here.

Thidrik's Saga addresses itself to the forging of *Mimming* by the demi-god Volund the Smith. The unlikely-sounding process involves making a complete sword, filing it into dust and feeding it to domestic fowl so that it becomes thoroughly mixed with their droppings. This cycle is carried out twice before Volund is satisfied with the results. Independent evidence for the use of a similar technique by the Rus (a people of Norse origin settled on the major rivers of what became Russia) appears in Arabic manuscripts. These stories may simply be misunderstandings of the use of animal dung in forging techniques, possibly to introduce trace elements of nitrates into the blade.

The most desirable trace element in a ferrous metal weapon is carbon. Iron cannot be hardened until it contains at least a 0.2 per cent carbon, at greater than 1 per cent carbon the compound is no longer steel. Viking smiths had to judge the amount of carbon by traditional methods handed down from previous masters. Barbarian smiths from the 2nd century BC onwards appear to have understood that the surface or iron could be carburised by exposure to carbon-based gases in a reducing atmosphere that excluded air. This could be achieved in a clay box containing carboniferous material at a high temperature.

Medium-quality steel for the forging of weapons could be produced by heating iron ore to 1200 degrees centigrade in a furnace alongside organic material such as bones. This could then be forged and drawn into rods with a steel surface. These could subsequently be twisted and forged with rods of lower carbon content into a composite blade giving a patterned appearance. This is the process sometimes called 'pattern-welding'.

Axes and spear heads were normally made from plain steel, although weapons of both these types have been found constructed by pattern-welding techniques. Edges of harder steel were sometimes welded to less brittle weapon bodies formed from steel of a lower carbon content.

Evidence for all stages of the weapon-making process from the most basic levels can be seen at the Viking site at Black Duck Brook site in Newfoundland. The archaeologist Helge Ingstad found evidence for the working of bog iron, a naturally occurring ferrous deposit on certain kinds of plant. The structure she identified as a smithy was at the extreme western limit of the known travels of the Vikings. This was part of a temporary settlement but was already capable of producing iron after what may have been only a few years' occupation.

The forging of the sword *Ekkisax*, by the dwarf Alberich, required the material of the blade to be

A rear view of a 'Great Polish' helmet clearly showing the four-plate construction with no frame. This example was originally gilded and probably also had a plume holder. (Liverpool City Museum, currently displayed in the Medieval Gallery of the White Tower at the Royal Armouries, Tower of London)

buried in the ground for some time to improve its quality. This may refer to the method of burying bog iron nodules to allow the non-ferrous inclusions to be absorbed out of the ore. After this period of curing, the remaining deposit could be worked into a thick bar at temperatures well below the melting point of iron. A lump of iron could be heated and squeezed to force out impurities in this way. Before modern metallurgical processes allowed the easy exploitation of haematite (an iron oxide ore), the majority of iron produced in Scandinavia was extracted in this way.

Armour production

Our knowledge of the armour production in the Viking Age is obscured by the lack of relevant finds from archaeological sites. Organic body armour is unknown except in later literary references and in art that is difficult to interpret. The surviving shields are almost entirely grave deposits whose organic components have usually rotted away, and were excavated at a time when archaeological practice was less rigorous.

The principal form of metallic armour used by the Viking warrior was mail. There are numerous references in Old Norse literature to this type of defence. The only known form in north-western Europe appears as a series of interlocking rings either butted, fixed with a rivet or made as a complete circle. The normal pattern of linking is four rings attached to each one. This can be increased or decreased to allow for variation in the shape of the wearer's body.

Each ring is made from a circle of ferrous metal, the use of copper alloy rings as a decorative border can be dated back securely no earlier than the 14th century. The wire of which the rings are formed has to be drawn through a series of successively smaller holes in a metal plate to achieve the required thickness. Recent research suggests that iron rich in phosphorous displays superior properties for drawing in this manner.

Repairing weapons

The maintenance of weapons falls into two categories: specialist attention, either in the field or workshop; and improvised repairs to broken weapons. The latter might be as simple as straightening a bent swordblade under one's foot. The Celts are described by classical authors as carrying this out in the midst of battle. The story is probably told as a comment on the poor workmanship of Celtic swordblades and also appears in several Icelandic sagas in this context. The character Steinthor in *Eyrbyggja Saga* is mocked during one combat for the weakness of his swordblade in a previous fight. Kjartan in *Laxdaela Saga* has a similar experience which actually leads to his death. *Kormak's Saga* tells how Kormak, a somewhat feckless young warrior, damages the edge of Skofnung (originally the sword of Hrolf Kraki, a king of Denmark) in combat. Attempting to resharpen the blade he makes matters worse by enlarging the size of the notch. A proper

Taken from the grave of a smith at Bygland, Morgedal, this group of Viking tools includes a ladle, sledgehammers, tongs, shears, an anvil and stakes for shaping metal. (Universitetets Oldsaksamling, Oslo)

▶ *This partly reconstructed Viking-age forge has several trade ingots of iron standing in the corner to the left and some fine metalworking hammers displayed above the anvil at centre right. The forge itself includes a bed of ard-stone and the diagram shows a double bellows. (Universitetets Oldsaksamling, Oslo)*

resharpening was a skilled undertaking. *Droplaugar-sona Saga* tells how a servant called Thorbjorn, known for his skill in the maintenance of weapons, was in the process of sharpening a sword for Helgi, one of the heroes of the saga. Grim, the brother of Helgi, later asks for this weapon in particular. Personal whetstones, in one case fitted with a suspension ring and small enough to have been worn as an amulet, have been found in Viking contexts. Olaf Tryggvason at the Battle of Svold was so concerned to ensure his men had sharp swords that he began an issue of new weapons in the midst of the fight.

Swords could be carried and re-used for generations, their significance and worth increasing as time passed. The value to the individual warrior was greater than that of a mere weapon. Ancient swords were status symbols and a nexus of power and influence. To the clan they could be a symbol of legitimacy intimately connected with luck and prosperity. Although the sagas speak of swords over two hundred years old being used in combat it can be assumed that great care would be taken of such items under normal circumstances.

Some ancient swords damaged beyond repair were re-forged into spearheads. Perhaps the best-known of these was *Grasida* or 'Greyflank' which is mentioned in the story of Gisli Surson. The useful life of 'Greyflank' as a sword came to an end when it broke in a fight. The metal of the original sword may

have been of sufficiently high quality to justify reforging it. It is possible that the fragments were thought to be charged with the virtue of the ancient blade. There was malign intent in the act of reforging: a sorcerer was specifically chosen for the task. An unusually short handle only eight inches long was provided for 'Greyflank' as a spear, a feature which may reflect some unknown ceremonial meaning. The pattern-welded weapon was then used in the murders of Vestein and Thorgrim.

MUSEUMS

British Museum
By far the best collection of Viking Age items in Britain. A tremendous variety of weapons but no helmets or mail shirts from this period. The collection of small finds is excellent, ranging from stirrups to pins. The Vikings Exhibition of 1980 saw the production of a useful catalogue. James Graham-Campbell and Dafydd Kidd, *The Vikings*, British Museum Publications, 1980. This details much Scandinavian and continental material rarely seen in this country.

Museum of London
Good collection of weapons and an extensive collection of other Viking finds. An early but valuable catalogue of some of the best-known items was

Although later than the Viking period, this 12th-century carving of a workshop scene shows an ard-stone, double bellows and a torch for the subdued lighting which allowed the smith to judge the state of the metal by radiant heat. This carving is from the west portico of Hylestad stave-church Setesdal, Norway.

▶ Few illustrations survive of Viking seaborne activity. However, this scene from the Bayeux Tapestry, showing horses being landed, is nearly contemporary and Viking methods probably differed little from those shown here. (With special permission of the town of Bayeux)

written by R.E.M. Wheeler, *London and the Vikings*, Museum of London, 1927.

Jorvik Centre/Archaeological Resource Centre, York
These are two separate museums, the first dedicated to the Viking settlement of Jorvik and the second an unusual glimpse into the various excavations in York. The Jorvik Centre includes a 'dark-ride' through a reconstructed section of the Coppergate area as it would have appeared in the middle of the 10th

century. This gives a vivid impression of everyday Viking life. The small museum attached to the centre has some of the best preserved textiles, shoes and small items in England. It should be borne in mind that civilian dress of this type would form the basic dress of the Viking warrior.

Scandinavian Museums

Statens Historiska Museum, Stockholm
Contains not only the major Swedish finds of the

Viking era, but also items from the earlier Vendel/Valsgarde culture. As with many Scandinavian museums, a fine collection of English silver coinage is also held.

Universitetets Oldsaksamling (Archaeology museum), Oslo
The major Viking collection in Norway. Includes the Gjermundbu helmet.

Viking ship Museum, Oslo
Holds the three impressive Viking ships from Oseberg, Gokstad and Tune, together with associated finds.

Nationalmuseet, Copenhagen
The largest collection of Danish material, not as impressive as the Swedish and Norwegian collections, but still of tremendous importance.

Vikingeskibshallen (Viking Ship Museum), Roskilde Denmark
Less than an hour from Copenhagen. Contains Viking vessels found in the Roskilde fjord. Several reconstructed ships and audio-visual displays.

COLLECTING

Original Viking Age weapons are often available on the open market. Swords are less common than spears and axeheads and attract the highest prices. All are relatively more expensive than medieval equivalents probably owing to the stronger images which attach to them. Condition is liable to be very poor, although some river finds can be remarkably well preserved due to a hard black patina which develops in anaerobic conditions. The frequency of river deposition appears to have increased during the period, possibly as Christianity was supplanted in certain areas of Britain by Norse religious practice. Care should be taken to familiarise oneself with the difference between swords of the early medieval era and 19th century Sudanese kaskaras. The latter are often mistaken for Viking blades. Specialist antique dealers in the field of arms and armour may hold items of interest but the two major auction houses, Sotheby's and Christie's are liable to be the best sources of original material

THE PLATES

A: Scandinavian warrior, 6th–7th Centuries
This figure is based on the spearmen depicted on the Torslunda plates from pre-Viking Sweden. The middle-status warrior we see here died over a hundred years before the attack on Lindisfarne and in that respect is an 'ancestor' of the Vikings.

The Torslunda plates were dies for decorating

the foil plaques used on helmets of the Vendel type. Their subject matter is ceremonial and mythical. The helmet worn by this proto-Viking could be covered with plates of the pictorial kind rather than the corrugated plaques shown. In either case they were held in position by strips of ribbed foil rivetted to the sub-frame. A fixed spectacle vizor would be a possible addition.

The cheek-pieces and neckguard identify the headgear firmly as Scandinavian, though the boar crest is similar to that found on the Anglian Benty Grange helmet. The Torslunda plaques show processional warriors in tunics with braided hems but

mail shirts would be likely in wartime. The sword is of the continental Migration Period form, with a hilt built up from metal and organic (wood, bone or antler) components. One of the Torslunda plaques depicts a naked man with a sword carried on a baldric like this one.

B: The Battle of Hafrsfjord c.872

Onund Treefoot is about to earn his nickname at the hands of an axe-armed Ulfhednar. While defending himself from a spear thrust during a boarding attempt the hero has 'blind-sided' himself with his own shield.

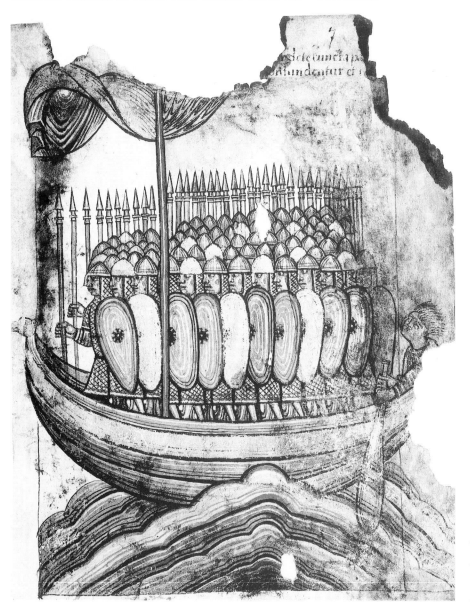

The seaborne warriors in this illustration from the 'Life of St. Aubin probably give a good impression of the appearance of the more 'professional' warriors of the later Viking age. (Bibliothèque Nationale, Paris)

Anglo-Norse Huscarls in action. The scene may represent swordsmen equipped with round shields, fighting in close co-operation with two-handed axemen. (Bayeux Tapestry. With special permission of the town of Bayeux)

The Ulfhednar are shown wearing distinctive wolf-skin capes. All the evidence for the wearing of full skins with the mask of the animal worn over the head is pre-Viking, scanty and possibly informed by legend and ceremonial costume.

Decorative figureheads may have been taken inboard during battles. The bows of a ship were considered the place of honour in such engagements.

Boarding was the main tactic in naval battles and the same weapon skills and small unit tactics were used on land.

An uncommitted squadron in the background has retained a level of initiative but once it is locked into the struggle the ability to manouvre can only be recovered by clearing the ships with which it is engaged.

C: Shields

The artefacts illustrated in this plate are all Scandinavian. Kite-shaped shields are not shown as they were late arrivals in Norse military fashion in the 11th century and were of continental origin. Most shields of the period were circular. The oval shield from the Oseberg Tapestry is uncorroborated by excavation. The closest comparison is the shield carried by the bearded huscarl in the Hastings section of the Bayeux Tapestry. The Oseberg example may be an accurate rendition given that the wheels of a cart on the same work are perfectly circular. The shield numbered 8 is an attempt to reinterpret the oval as a circular form.

Each of the objects shown includes some form of boss and a rim. Number 3 is unusual in that the rim is formed of ferrous metal. Such fittings were more usually of leather, hardened by boiling, which were nailed or sewn into position. Shields could have unfaced fronts with the boards simply painted as in 2 (a Gokstad shield) or covered with leather. Leather facings were a single circular sheet or pieces cut to a spiral form and sewn together. In both cases these were usually painted, perhaps in variegated colours.

Motifs on shields could indicate the bearer's intentions, like the red war-shield (4), or even identify the owner and his affiliations. Bosses were hemispherical or cone-shaped. The edges of the circular boss could be shaped with indentations like those from the Viking burial on the Ile-de-Groix.

D: Training

This reconstruction of a training session at Jomsberg shows the *skjaldborg* (shield-wall) arranged in a mutually supporting double line. The kneeling men protect the legs of the standing second rank who in turn cover the heads of the front rank. The archer in the background has sought to find gaps in the shield wall to shoot his headless arrows through. These still have penetrating power, and some are lodged in shields. Failure to maintain an arrow-proof defence could prove painful for the careless 'trainee'.

A senior Jomsviking has chosen this moment to test the strength of the *skjaldborg* by attempting to kick one of the trainees out of position. He is a person of some status, as indicated by his silver-inlaid axe and gold arm-ring contrasting with the relative simplicity of his dress.

E: The Battle of Brunanburh

The ferocity of Viking of hand-to-hand combat is captured in this reconstruction of the Battle of Brunanburh. In the foreground opposing *skjaldborgs* are meeting in an onset of two swine arrays. Employing a combination of spears and secondary weapons the two *aetts* are attempting to push back or kill their opponents and penetrate the enemy formation. The battlefield was the ultimate test of the bonds of kinship, artificial or otherwise, within a warrior group.

The similarity of equipment is not surprising as Vikings fought on both sides in this engagement. The tactics employed are also identical, with shields overlapping to almost half their width. The ability of the combatants to maintain this posture was affected by the speed of advance and variation in terrain. Archers are posted to the rear of the shield wall where they can contribute by overhead shooting. Thrown spears or javelins might be employed in the same way.

An English unit on the hillock in the mid-ground has been overrun by a unit of Strathclyde Britons.

The followers of King Athelstan had been separated from their supporting *skjaldborg* in an earlier advance. The Britons are in a triumphant mood and have even begun to strip the corpses of the slain.

Anglo-Norse Huscarls under combined cavalry and missile attack. The axeman is using an axe, apparently of Petersen type M, left handed. (Bayeux Tapestry. With special permission of the town of Bayeux)

The shield wall at Hastings, formed of heavily equipped men using kite-shaped shields. A single archer provides missile support. From Stothard's 'Bayeux Tapestry', 1819, Plate 14.

F: Viking Warriors, 8th–9th Centuries

The warrior shown here is of the *hersir* class at the height of the Nordic threat to Europe. His status is distinguished by his ownership of helmet, gold arm-ring and decorated sword. Non-Christian beliefs are revealed by the hammer-shaped amulet, although caution might lead the Viking to worship Christ on land and Thor when at sea.

The red tunic is dyed with an extract from the roots of the plant *Rubia tinctorum*. His trousers are of undyed wool. His cloak was made in Iceland and is a dark-coloured version of *wadmal* cloth.

Our subject normally keeps his beard and hair carefully combed but is, at present, a little wind-swept. His sax or knife is influenced by English fashion. The sword, though decorated, is nonetheless a practical weapon. Its long cutting edges are most suited to deliver effective slashes against unarmoured men.

The warrior is not shown wearing a byrnie as he is not preparing for a full scale battle. Instead he has left his armour in storage, preferring increased mobility in the task that faces him.

The shield is constructed from thin planks held together at the rear by a transverse extended grip and bound at the edges by a rim of hardened leather.

G: Weaponsmith's workshop

This view of a Viking Age atelier illustrates most of the items needed by a smith for the production of arms and armour. The building is constructed from stout uprights supporting horizontal planks and is open to the front for ventilation. The interior is fairly gloomy, lit by the glow of the forge and a single, wall mounted 'cresset' filled with fish-oil and a burning wick. Low light levels allow the craftsman to judge processes by radiant heat. Water for quenching is kept in the bucket to the right of the forge.

The forge is made of piled turf with a bed of charcoal on the upper surface. The heat is controlled by currents of air from the bellows. The draught is channelled through a so-called *ard* of soapstone carved with the face of Loki, which protects the bellows from extreme heat. Balanced on the edge of the forge, at convenient working height, are the tools of the smith's trade. These include rasps, tongs and a selection of hammers.

Next to the forge stands a tree stump cut to balance firmly on the packed dirt or clay floor. A hollow is cut into the top of this log for the beating out of bosses and helmet components. Two anvils are mounted nearby, one a solid block and the other a robust right angle. A 'steel' of high carbon iron, from which the workman lights his forge striking sparks with a flint, lies on the anvil bed. A much larger anvil, a massive water-worn boulder, appears to the left of the stump with two sledgehammers leaning against it.

The table is taken up by a square ladle (for the casting of high-value metals), a clay brooch mould, and a group of partly finished knifeblades. A metal

H: Swords and axes

The seven-part typology proposed by R.E.M. Wheeler is outlined in the 'ghost' images arranged around figure 8 on this plate. No strict chronology underlies Wheeler's ideas, which concentrate on the structure of the hilt rather than shape of the blade. Type I is often seen as an earlier form, lacking the decorative pommel cap interpreted as a representational reliquary bag by some authorities. The simplicity of design may be governed by the smith's need to complete a job quickly. Type II corresponds to Petersen's Type C. Petersen sees this as being an early form. The pommels of long-saxes are usually in this category.

Many sword hilts were intricately and richly decorated like 9, 10 and 14 with precious metal foil plates and inlay. The blades of axes are less frequently embellished to this extent. Distinctive decoration probably marks out weapon as opposed to tool axes as in the case of 2 and 6.

Broader-bladed axes are a late development characterised by 2 and 3. The dagged projections around the sides of the socket would serve the practical purpose of spreading lines of force and protecting the axehead from shearing off its wooden haft. Hafts could be bound with a copper alloy sheath extending some way below the head.

I: Spears and javelins

Many spearheads recovered from levels of the 8th and 11th centuries in Scandinavia are of foreign origin. The type with wings mounted on the socket are generally taken to be Carolingian. The Finnish spearhead, numbered 1, appears to be an indigenous product, 2 is Norwegian and possibly of local manufacture. Both might be influenced by imports like 11 and 12.

The broad-bladed decorated spear at 10 is reminiscent of earlier Celtic styles but is, apparently, of Viking date. Such a wide-bladed spear would be most useful for a stabbing attack but, *in extremis* and at short range, it could be thrown. 3 and 4 represent a common intermediate form between javelin and thrusting spear. 15 and 16 are specialised javelins found in Norway. 17, 18 and 19 are said to be arrowheads but as the shortest item in this group measures over four inches the entire series might be best interpreted as light javelins.

This 12th-century armoured figure, though wearing the divided mail-shirt of a cavalryman, gives a good idea of the appearance of the late Viking warrior. The conical helmet is apparently forged in one piece. The supporting 'guige-strap' of the kite-shaped shield is clearly visible. (Cast of the font of Hildesheim cathedral)

plate pierced with holes, through which wire can be drawn lies near a surprisingly modern-looking hacksaw.

The tools in this illustration are based on those from the Mastermyar tool-chest. A version of this last item can be seen in the shadows against the wall. Helmets, shields and swords in various stages of construction are also visible. To the extreme right of the scene are piles of charcoal and slag (from bog-iron production) along with ingots and imported iron in the form of crude axe or spear heads.

Spearshafts were always of wood, most often ash. Written records inform us that the hafts of spears might be bound with iron but this is not confirmed by the archaeological record.

J: Helmets

The *spangenhelm* from Chalon-sur-Saône represents the Germanic method of helmet construction of the late classical period. This derives ultimately from Central Asian techniques. The Chalons helmet is built up from six inverted T-shaped members attaching to a brow band at the base and meeting in a disc fitting at the crown. The spaces between this framework are filled by shaped metal plates.

The Giecz helmet, of 'Great Polish' form, dates from approximately 450 years after the Chalons spangenhelm but perpetuates broadly similar methods. The four plates which make up the Giecz example are wider and more complex in shape. The uprights are dispensed with. An appliqué brow piece is attached to the front plate. A conical helmet with nasal made in a simlar way and described as Northern French is displayed in the Metropolitan Museum in New York. The Sigtuna elk antler carving may be a representation of the same type of head defence. Although the Gjermundbu helmet has features reminiscent of much older Scandinavian forms it was made in a similar way to the *spangenhelm* series.

Conical helmets in the Central European fashion appear in the Olmütz-Poznań-Wenceslas series. These are formed from a single piece of metal except the Wenceslas helmet which displays several unusual features. The point of the dome is comparatively low, a medial keel follows the centre line (giving greater rigidity to the structure) and a combined brow band and nasal is fitted being silvered and decorated with a crucifixion and knotwork motif.

The diagram of the lacing of lamellar armour shows how the Birka plates were originally articulated. Long laces could be cut as a spiral from leather of suitable thickness. In reality the thongs would be pulled together more tightly causing the plates to overlap in all directions.

K: Viking Fort

This Danish fortress, typical of the 'Trelleborg' series features the precise layout of the main hall structures, arranged in fours around the side of a square. Each group of four is positioned within a quadrant of the characteristic circular rampart. Like all known sites of this type the fort is situated near a great water feature. The principal means of communication for this defensive system was water-borne. The emergence of such structures was a feature of growing royal power in Denmark.

The large halls reflect the Scandinavian concept of military organisation. Long houses of this type were a centre of power where wealth could be gathered and redistributed to the immediate retainers of a king, who were the basis of his ability to control his realm. The best known hall was called *Heorot*, the hall of King Hrothgar in the early poem *Beowulf*.

By the time of the 'Trelleborg' forts the permanent presence of the monarch was no longer vital. A king's followers were able to gather in one place and use the resources of the surrounding region to carry on the business of government.

The close link between warfare and society in Denmark at this time meant that a separate military authority did not exist. The addition of specialised buildings such as workshops, stores and stables allowed the operation of these forts as economic and military centres.

L: Viking Warrior, 10th–11th Centuries

By this period the character of fighting men of middle rank had undergone remarkable changes. The *hersir* had ceased to be an independent figure in the Norse states, legitimised by wealth, power and ancestry. Instead he was now a representative of royal authority. The legal force which now supported him was regal, national and backed by Christianity. The increased wealth of royal power, through its monopoly of taxation allowed the creation of a new middle class of warrior. This theory of military service had developed from much older concepts of shared kinship, common purpose and benevolent dependency.

Both the local leader and the retained bodyguard could be expected to appear for war equipped like this figure. The helmet is a high domed version of the Wenceslas type (it may be a Central European import). The mail coif, lined with leather at the edges for greater comfort, is a continental influence.

The rest of his warrior's equipment is Scandinavian, in particular the long-handled axe with the

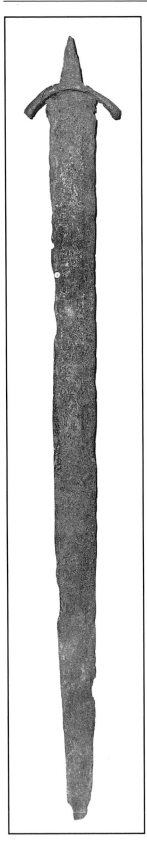

broad blade. The three-lobed pommel of the sword indicates it is an heirloom, but still sound in combat and valuable as a status item. The shield is also a little archaic for the last fifty years of the period but preferred by the user to the kite-shaped alternative. The mail shirt may be non-Scandinavian being forked to divide between the legs, allowing the wearer to ride in full gear. A Huscarl of this date might be expected to ride to battle if not actually fight as a cavalryman.

Further reading

Many of the most useful books on the subject are long out of print, but given that the majority of relevant information was known at the turn of the century, some of these more venerable works are still of value.

Haakon Shetelig (ed.), *Viking Antiquities in Great Britain and Ireland* (Oslo, 1940), in six volumes.
Jan Petersen, *De Norske Vikingesverd: En typologisk-kronologisk studie over vikigetidens vaaben* (Kristiana, 1919)
Bertil Almgren (ed.), *The Viking* (Vitoria, 1975)
P. G. Foote & D. M. Wilson, *The Viking Achievement* (Sidgwick and Jackson, 1970)
D. M. Wilson, *The Vikings and their Origins*, (Thames and Hudson, 1970)
J. Brøndsted, *The Vikings* (Penguin, 1960)
N. F. Blake (Trans), *The Saga of the Jomsvikings* (Thomas Nelson and Sons, 1962)
Samuel Laing (Trans), *The Heimskringla* (J. M. Dent and Sons, 1930), in three volumes.
Gwyn Jones, *A History of the Vikings* (Oxford University Press, 1968)
James Graham-Campbell, *The Viking World* (Frances Lincoln, 1980)
H. R. Lyon, *The Vikings in Britain*, (1977)
Magnus Magnusson & Hermann Pálsson (Trans), *Njal's Saga*, (1971)

◄◄*Badly corroded sword found near Mortimer's Cross, Shropshire. Despite the loss of the pommel, it is still identifiable as of Petersen type L, by the downward curve of the quillons. (Ludlow Museum, Shropshire)*

◄*This type X broadsword, which appears in the 10th and 11th centuries, is one of the latest classifiable by Petersen's typology. Later models are classified by blade profile rather than pommel design. (Royal Armouries, Tower of London)*

Jacqueline Simpson, *Everyday Life in the Viking Age*, (1967)

Michael Wood, *In Search of the Dark Ages*, (1981)

R. T. Farrell (ed.), *The Vikings*, (1982) Ian Atkinson, *The Viking Ships*, (1980)

GLOSSARY

Amulet An ornament or piece of jewellery worn for good luck and to ward off evil.

Berserker A particularly fanatical (and perhaps psychotic) Viking warrior.

Boss The metal guard covering the hand-grip of a shield.

Carburised iron A soft impure form of steel.

Coif An item of head protection, usually a mail hood.

Fyrd The territorial levy of an Anglo-Saxon region.

Garniture A set of armour with additional pieces which can be added or discarded according to necessity.

Hersir Scandinavian local leader. The word derives from *here*, a military host. Originally a freeholder but later becoming a form of royal official.

Hilt The 'handle' of a sword consistng of the cross-guard, grip and pommel.

Hird The territorial levy of a Scandinavian region.

Jarl Scandinavian regional ruler, usually the immediate subordinate of a king but sometimes independent.

Lamellar A type of armour made of small metal strips laced together.

Mail Armour made from large numbers of small, interlinked iron rings.

Pattern-welding A method of weapon manufacture by twisting rods of iron and carburised iron.

Pommel The weighted end of a sword hilt, used to help counterbalance the blade.

Reeve Anglo-Saxon minor royal official.

Sax A single-edged knife of anything up to sword length. Usually with a back thicker than the edge; the back often has an angled profile.

Skjalborg (shield-wall). A tightly arrayed body of warriors who are close enough to overlap shields in a mutually defensive barrier.

Svinfylka (swine-array). An offensive formation of warriors fighting in a wedge shape.

Varangian Guard The personal bodyguard of the Byzantine Emperor which initially consisted entirely of Scandinavian warriors.

Vinland The name given by the Vikings to America.

Notes sur les planches en couleurs

A Guerrier scandinave de rang moyen, VIᶜ–VIIᶜ siècle. C'est l'ancêtre du guerrier viking traditionnel. La silhouette de cet homme est inspirée des découvertes archéologiques portant sur la periode de la culture de Valsgärde/Vendel. Les protège-joues comme le couvre-nuque sont typiquement scandinaves.

B Le combat au corps à corps, véritable duel, était la règle lors des bataille navales. Les vaisseaux, bord à bord, après l'abordage s'empêchaient mutuellement toute autre manoeuvre. Cette saynète représente un des *berserks* (littéralement: chemise d'ours) ou *Ulfhednar* (peau de loup) du roi Harald de Norvège; il est revêtu de la traditionnelle peau de loup. De sa hache il se prépare à couper la jambe d'Onund – qui sera, après cet épisode, surnommé «*pied d'arbre*».

C Jusqu'à ce que la mode se généralise, au XIᶜ siècle, du bouclier en forme d'écu allongé, les boucliers vikings sont circulaires. Réalisés en bois, recouverts de cuir, il possède en leur centre un ombo de métal. Rien ne prouve la généralisation d'un cerclage extérieur en métal. C4 «Bouclier de guerre» utilisé lors d'une des expéditions américaines, peint en rouge symbole d'intentions hostiles. C8 Un bouclier semi-oval représenté sur la tapisserie d'Oseberg; nous l'avons redessiné, à droite, dans sa forme circulaire plus conventionnelle.

D Séance d'entraînement à Jomsberg, cantonnement des *Jomsvikings*, guerriers semi-permanents. Ces guerriers à l'exercice forment le *Skjaldborg* (mur de boucliers), formation tactique qui n'est pas sans rappeler la tortue romaine où les boucliers des hommes du premier rang, agenouillés, protègent efficacement les jambes de ceux du second rang des flèches ennemies. Un vétéran teste la solidité du mur.

E Deux *Skjaldborgs* s'affrontent à la bataille de Brunanburh, Angleterre, en 937 après Jésus Christ. L'équipement défensif et l'armement de chaque armée sont identiques, les Vikings se battant dans les deux camps.

F Un guerrier *hersir*, catégorie élévée dans la classe guerrière scandinave (VIIIᶜ–IXᶜ

Farbtafeln

A Ein skandinavischer Krieger mittleren Ranges aus dem 6.–7. Jahrhundert. Er ist ein Vorfahre des Wikinger und die Abbildung beruht auf archäologischen Funden vom Ende der Valsgärde/Vendel-Periode. Die Backenstücke und der Nackenschutz seines Helms sind unverwechselbar skandinavisch.

B Die gängigste Taktik bei den Seeschlachten der Wikinger war der Kampf von Mann zu Mann: für gewöhnlich blockierten sich die Schiffe gegenseitig und wunden somit manövrierunfähig. Die Abbildung zeigt einen der *Berserker* ('Bärenhemden') oder *Ulfhednar* ('Wolfsfelle') des König Harald von Norwegen. Er trägt das bezeichnende Wolfsfell. Er wird sogleich mit seiner Axt das Bein von Onund – der später den Beinamen 'Baumfuß' erhielt – abtrennen.

C Bis im 11. Jahrhundert drachenförmige Schilde in Mode kamen, waren die Schilde der Wikinger fast alle rund. Sie waren aus Holz, das mit Leder überzogen war, und hatten in der Mitte einen Schildbuckel aus Metall. Es gibt so gut wie kein Beweismaterial für Schildränder aus Metall. Bei C4 handelt es sich um einen 'Kriegsschild' von den Expeditionen nach Amerika, der rot angemalt ist um feindliche Absichten anzukündigen. C8 zeigt einen halbovalen Schild von der Oseberg Tapestry; wir rekonstruiren dies als einen normalen, runden Schild.

D Ausbildungsübung in Jomsberg, dem Standort der halbberuflichen Jomswikinger. Die angehenden Krieger stellen sich in einem *Skjaldborg* (Schildwall) auf, wobei die Schilde der Männer im vorderen Rang die Beine derer im zweiten Rang decken und somit einen pfeilsicheren Schutz bieten. Ein altgedienter Jomswikinger prüft die Stärke des Walls.

E Zwei gegnerische *Skjaldborgs* treffen bei der Schlacht von Brunanburh in England, ca. 937 n. Chr. aufeinander. Die Ausrüstung der beiden Armeen gleicht sich, da die Wikinger auf beiden Seiten kämpften.

F Ein Krieger der *Hersir*-Klasse aus dem 8.–9. Jahrhundert zur Zeit, als die Überfälle der Wikinger auf Europa ihren Höhepunkt erreicht hatten. Sein hoher

63

siècle), à l'époque où les raids vikings en Europe occidentale sont à leur apogée. Son statut élevé est reconnaissable à son casque, son bracelet et son épée richement travaillée.

G Une forge viking. Le foyer, tapissé de charbon de bois, est réalisé sur un socle élevé de tourbe. Deux gros soufflets de forge sont utilisés pour attiser les flammes. Le forgeron-armurier et ses soufflets sont protégés de la chaleur par une pierre *ard*, représentant le dieu Loki. Deux enclumes sont incrustées dans une grosse souche dont la partie droite est évidée pour permettre la mise en forme, par martelage, des casques et des ombos de boucliers. Les outils sont inspirés de ceux trouvés dans le coffre de Mastermyar.

H L'épée viking est une arme longue et droite, à double tranchant, plus employée pour frapper de taille que d'estoc. Les haches aux fers larges, et utilisées à deux mains, ne seront généralisées qu'à la fin de la période viking classique. La plupart de celles maniées par les Vikings étaient du type à une main. Les épées et les haches des Vikings de haut rang étaient richement décorées.

I Au combat les guerriers vikings utilisaient plus la lance que l'épée. De nombreux fers de lances possédaient à l'embase des «arrêts» empêchant l'arme de pénétrer trop profondément dans le corps de l'adversaire, cette disposition fut probablement empruntée après les nombreux contacts que les Vikings eurent avec l'empire de Charlemagne. **I 15–I 19** Ces fers sont probablement tous utilisés avec des javelines pour le jet.

J Le seul casque pouvant être attribué avec certitude à la production armurière viking est celui provenant du site de Gjermundbu (**J1**). Ce type de coiffure est très proche de celui appelé *Spangenhelm* (**J5, J7**), très fréquent sur de nombreux sites en Europe. Les Vikings portaient volontiers de nombreux types de casque provenant, ou inspirés, d'Europe Centrale (**J2, J3, J8**). Cette armure, découverte sur le site de Birka en Suède, faite de petites plaques de métal liées les unes aux autres par des cordonnets de cuir (**J9**), demeure un exemple unique de ce type de protection en Scandinavie. Elle est probablement importée d'Europe de l'est.

K Un fort danois du type de *Trelleborg*. Sa forme circulaire est caractéristique. Quatre groupes de quatre habitations sont disposés en carré, chacun dans un des quarts du cercle. Ces forts, à cette période, sont toujours construits près d'une rivière, un lac ou en bord de mer.

L Guerrier viking du Xe–XIe siècle. A cette époque, le *hersir* n'est plus un chef de guerre indépendant; il a vu son rôle réduit à celui de membre de la maison royale, proche de l'emploi, du statut, d'un *huscarl* de la bataille d'Hastings. Si son casque est typiquement d'Europe centrale, son équipement, son armement et ses vêtements sont typiquement scandinaves.

Rang ist durch seinen Helm, den goldenen Armring und das verzierte Schwert ersichtlich.

G Werkstatt eines Waffenschmieds der Wikinger. Die Esse besteht aus mehreren Lagen Sode um ein Holzkohlenbett. Mit Blasebalgen kann die Temperatur gesteigert werden. Sie sind durch einen *Ard*-Stein, in den das Gesicht des Gottes Loki gemeißelt ist, vor der Hitze geschützt. Ein großer Baumstumpf mit zwei Ambössen und einer ausgehöhlten Vertiefung dient zum Aushämmern von Helmen und Schildbuckeln. Die Werkzeuge beruhen auf denjenigen, die in der Mastermyar-Truhe gefunden wurden.

H Das gängigste Wikinger-Schwert war lang und gerade und hatte eine zweischneidige Klinge. Es war eher zum Schneiden als zum Zustechen gedacht. Äxte mit breiten Klingen, die mit beiden Händen geschwungen wurden, wurden erst gegen Ende der Wikingerzeit verwendet; meistens handelte es sich um einfache, einhändige Modelle. Die Schwerter und Äxte der wohlhabenderen Wikinger waren sehr reich verziert.

I Speere waren viel gängiger als Schwerter. Viele der Speerspitzen der Wikinger hatten 'Flügel', die ein tiefes Eindringen des Speers in das Opfer verhinderten – diese wurden wahrscheinlich aus dem Heiligen Römischen Reich Karl des Großen eingeführt. Bei **I 15–I 19** handelt es sich wahrscheinlich um Wurfspieße.

J Der einzige Helm, der sich mit Sicherheit den Wikingern zuschreiben läßt, ist der aus Gjermundbu (**J1**). Er ähnelt in der Gestaltung dem *Spangenhelm*, der auf dem europäischen Festland vorkam (**J5, J7**). Auch scheinen die Wikinger Helme eingeführt zu haben, wie etwa die in Mitteleuropa auftretenden Modelle (**J2, J3, J8**). In Birka in Schweden fand man ein einzigartiges Beispiel einer Schuppenrüstung (**J9**), die unter Umständen aus dem Osten eingeführt worden war.

K Dänische Festung des Typs 'Trelleborg'. Die Anlagenform ist bezeichnenderweise rund. Die Gebäude sind jeweils in Vierergruppen um ein Quadrat angeordnet, und jede Gruppe liegt innerhalb eines Viertelkreises. Die Festungen dieser Zeit befanden sich stets in der Nähe eines Flusses, eines Sees oder des Meeres.

L Wikingerkrieger aus dem 10.–11. Jahrhundert. Zu dieser Zeit war der *Hersir* bereits kein unabhängiger Häuptling mehr, sondern lediglich ein Mitglied des königlichen Hofes – in Rang und Aufmachung ähnelt er einem *Huscarl*, der 1066 in der Schlacht von Hastings kämpfte. Sein Helm stammt wahrscheinlich aus Mitteleuropa, doch der Rest seiner Ausrüstung ist skandinavischer Herkunft.